- It's a kitchen basic tool.
- It's practical experience summed up.
- It's nutritional know-how charted.
- It's a fast reference in a cooking crisis.

THE BUSY COOK'S LOOK-IT-UP BOOK

CONSULT it before you shop. It informs you about meat grades, can sizes, signs of ripeness and spoilage, quality or waste.

CHECK it to explain an unfamiliar term your recipe uses or find a substitute for a hard-to-get ingredient.

REFER to it for flavor ideas to make everyday dishes exotic or create recipes of your own.

FOLLOW its time and temperature guides for the size and weight of food you need.

EQUIP your kitchen with the proper utensils. It describes both essentials and gadgets.

LEARN about wines . . . when to use them and at what temperatures to serve them.

EACH CHAPTER IS ARRANGED ALPHABETICALLY FOR QUICK AND EASY REFERENCE.

SIGNET Cook Books

The Busy Cook's
LOOK-IT-UP *Book*

by Dodi Schultz

A SIGNET BOOK

Published by
THE NEW AMERICAN LIBRARY

SIGNET TRADEMARK REG. U.S. PAT. OFF. AND FOREIGN COUNTRIES
REGISTERED TRADEMARK—MARCA REGISTRADA
HECHO EN CHICAGO, U.S.A.

SIGNET BOOKS are published by
The New American Library, Inc.,
1301 Avenue of the Americas, New York, New York 10019

FIRST PRINTING, MAY, 1969

PRINTED IN THE UNITED STATES OF AMERICA

Contents

The Busy Cook's
LOOK-IT-UP *Book*

I. How to Use This Book

You will not find a single recipe in this book—though you will find a number of helpful cooking hints. You will also find explanations of the culinary terms that may appear in your recipes; how long to roast meats, and at what temperature; how to choose the herbs to season the meat; how to shop for the vegetables; which wine to serve. Plus . . .

Well, it's unlikely you'll consult every chapter in this book for each meal you prepare. But hypothetically, let's say some special guests are coming to dinner. Naturally, you've already equipped your kitchen (Chapter XI). Now the first problem is shopping. You'll want to be sure there's enough to go around (Chapter IX), that the meat you plan to roast is top quality (Chapter III), and that the vegetables are nice and fresh (Chapter IV). If you do your shopping a day or two before, you'll want to be sure everything stays in good condition (Chapter V).

When it comes to the cooking, you'll want to pick the perfect flavorings for all your menu items (Chapter VI), and to be sure the roast is cooked at the right temperature for the right amount of time (Chapter VIII). After deglazing the pan (Chapter II), you find that you should boil the drippings (Chapter II) down to one gill, according to your British cookbook (Chapter VII), and thicken them with flour in order to make the gravy. You are fresh out of flour, you suddenly discover at the last minute, and need a substitute (Chapter X).

Naturally, you want to be sure to serve an absolutely correct wine with the meal (Chapter XII), and a dessert that will achieve a good nutritional balance (Chapter XIII). Then you learn that one of your guests is on a low-cholesterol diet, and of course you must make sure that all major menu items will be suitable for him (Chapter XIV). The guests come and everything goes splendidly—until someone spills a bit of the gravy on his lapel, and you must rush to the rescue (Chapter XV).

We've picked an admittedly unlikely combination of coincidences for our illustration. Point is, this is the book that backs up all your other cookbooks—the indispensable companion piece that removes the guesswork and lets you use your recipes to optimal advantage. It's a book we wish we'd had in our kitchen many years ago—and that, in fact, is where and when *The Busy Cook's Look-It-Up Book* began.

II.   The ABC's of Cookery

In this chapter you will find a potpourri of cooking terms, more or less defined, and accompanied in a number of instances by hints, suggestions, and miscellaneous information the author thinks may be helpful. A few terms of foreign derivation are included, but only those most likely to pop up perplexingly in American cookbooks.

À La . . .:   in the style or way of, and usually followed (except in the cases of the two terms below) by the name of a country, region, person, or culinary establishment. For example, **à la Française,** in the French manner; *à l'Alsacienne,* Alsation style; *à la Max's Delicatessen,* the special way Max does it; all indicate the presumed origin of the recipe or manner of preparation. Sometimes, confusingly, in some French dishes that find their way into Stateside recipe collections, the term replaces the word "with"—as in *Canard à l'Orange* (duck with orange) or anything *à la Crême* (with cream).

À La King: heated and served in a creamy sauce.

À La Mode: literally, in style or fashion, but idiomatically used in American cuisine to mean either of two very specific things. Referring to a main dish, such as a meat, it means the food is marinated, then usually cooked in the marinade as well. An *à la mode* dessert, usually pie or cake, is topped with or accompanied by a scoop of ice cream.

Aspic: a jelly or gelatinized fruit or vegetable served in or as a main or side dish, rather than as a dessert; often a gelled stock, which may or may not contain chopped meat, vegetables, or other foods. An aspic—tomato aspic, for example—frequently plays a major role in salads. Also used to describe a dish for which the main ingredient—as, fish—is coated with such a gelatin.

Au Gratin: cooked in a sauce and topped with cheese, or bread crumbs and butter, or both, the topping browned in the oven or under the broiler to form a light crust. An *au gratin* dish is usually served in its cooking container, a casserole or baking dish.

Bake: to cook by dry heat, as in an oven; technically, the same as "roast," but the latter term is normally reserved for large cuts of meat or whole fowl.

When baking potatoes, make a tiny slit in the skin before putting in the oven, to keep the potato from getting all steamed up inside and "exploding."

Test most cakes for doneness by slipping a toothpick into the center; if it comes out clean, the cake's done (see Chapter VIII for additional tests).

Barbecue: to roast slowly on a spit or rack, usually over coals or open flame outdoors (but sometimes via electric heat in a device designed to simulate the effect), and often basting with a highly seasoned sauce during cooking. Also, a picnic or outing featuring food cooked this way.

Baste: to moisten food with a liquid—melted fat, sauce, juices of the food itself, or other specified liquid—at intervals during cooking. Basting may be done with a spoon, a brush (as in barbecuing), or a baster. The last is especially handy for basting with juice or drippings too shallow to spoon up easily.

Batter: a mixture of flour, liquid, and other ingredients, to be cooked by baking (as, cakes) or frying (as, pancakes).

Beat: to stir vigorously and rapidly with a circular, lifting motion in order to incorporate air in a substance (as, eggs) or to insure thorough, smooth mixing of ingredients (as, cake batter). Beating may be done with a spoon or fork (for very light beating), or with a wire whisk, rotary beater, or electric beater.

Egg whites beat best, producing more volume (thus an airier or lighter result in the finished dish), if they are at room temperature. Try to take your eggs out of the refrigerator well before they're to be used. If your recipe calls for whites only, separate the eggs right away, leaving the whites out and returning the yolks to the refrigerator in a small jar or covered dish; if whole eggs are to be used, then just let them sit, unseparated (being at room temperature won't do anything special for the yolks, but it won't hurt them, either).

To add a little more body to beaten egg whites, beat in a little sugar—a teaspoon or two—near the end of the beating.

If your recipe specifies egg yolks beaten with sugar, and the mixture's then to be heated or cooked, add the sugar very gradually and beat only until, when you lift your beater, the yolk forms a definite ribbon. Overbeating could cause graininess in the mixture later.

When you're beating something thick and cold—a batter, for example—prevent sticking by heating your beater blades in hot water first.

Bisque: a thick, creamy soup, often—but not necessarily —made of shellfish such as crab or lobster.

Blanch: to plunge into boiling water briefly, then remove (sometimes instantly, sometimes after a minute or two) and place immediately in cold water to halt cooking, then drain. Also, to place in cold water, bring to a boil, then remove immediately from heat, etc. Food is usually blanched to pre-soften it prior to subsequent cooking, to facilitate skin removal (as with certain nuts, fruits and vegetables) or to temper an especially strong taste or odor.

Blend: to combine two or more ingredients in a thorough mixture; blending does not necessarily involve beating.

Boil: to bring a liquid to boiling temperature (for water, 212° F.) and to maintain it at that temperature for the specified length of time (so long as it is bubbling constantly, it is boiling); to cook a food in boiling liquid.

When boiling eggs, take them out of the refrigerator about half an hour ahead of time; that way, they're less apt to crack during the boiling. In any event, put some salt in the water to further discourage cracking, prevent the insides from leaking out if cracks do occur; bear in mind, too, that it needn't be a violent boil, just so long as the water's bubbling. Once they're done, soft-boiled eggs should be instantly removed from the heat, the boiling water poured off, and several fast cold-water rinses applied; otherwise, cooking will continue and the eggs will be hard-boiled.

How you boil meats or vegetables depends on your flavor aims. To seal in the food's own juices, bring the water to a boil, then add the food. To flavor your cooking liquid, draw out the food juices by placing the food in cold water, then heating the water to the boil.

Green vegetables keep their color and flavor best if they're boiled in an uncovered pot (and do be careful not to overcook—the just-tender point is when to stop). Red vegetables such as beets, on the other hand, are best boiled beneath a lid; a little lemon juice added near the end of the cooking will help their color and flavor, too. To subtly perk up the flavor of many vegetables, add a bouillon cube, a dash of herbs (see Chapter VI), or a pinch of sugar.

Be sure, when you're boiling frozen vegetables, to use a timer and cook them for the precise number of minutes the package directs; the slightest overcooking can cause a big drop in quality.

Bouillon: a pure broth or stock traditionally made from beef, but sometimes from poultry, fish, or vegetables; also available commercially in concentrate form.

A bouillon cube or packet of powder popped into the water in which you're boiling vegetables or rice can add interesting flavor; include it, too, in soups and stews for meatier taste.

Bouquet Garni: a combination of several herbs tied together and used to flavor a stew or other long-cooking dish; for further discussion, see Chapter VI.

Braise: to brown quickly in fat, then cook fairly slowly at low heat (either in the oven or on top of the stove) in a covered container, sometimes with added liquid, seasonings, and/or other ingredients; used for meats, as well as for some vegetables.

Bread: to coat with bread crumbs, prior to baking, browning, or frying; usually, the food is dipped into a liquid first (eggs, milk, fruit juice) to insure that the crumbs will stick.

Broil: to cook by direct exposure of the food to the source of heat, whether above or below—flame, coals, or electric heat. (Also see PAN-BROIL.)

Steaks and chops are the usual cuts of meat cooked by broiling (of course ground-meat patties, frankfurters, and fish fillets may be cooked this way, too). Be sure to slash the surrounding fat at about 1½-inch intervals to prevent curling up. Whatever a recipe may say, broiling time depends on your own tastes, on whether you like meat rare, medium, or well-done. Preheat your broiler. Check at intervals of a minute or two, cutting into the meat if necessary, and remember that the second side will cook faster than the first, since the second has already been exposed to the heat indirectly.

Broth: a thin soup or stock, which may or may not contain added meat or vegetables.

Brown: as a kitchen-proficient friend of the author is fond of explaining to culinary novices, brown is a color. Of, specifically, the surface of the food that has been thus treated. In the absence of other instructions, this word occurring in a recipe means that the food in question is to be cooked in a pan on top of the stove in a small amount of melted fat until the desired condition is achieved (and no longer—since this step usually precedes other cooking). "Brown quickly" means that the heat should be high.

Generally speaking—and, again, in the absence of specific instructions—something to be browned should be as dry as possible (i.e., drained or blotted with paper towels) before the browning. The fat should be as hot as possible before the food is put into it, and a combination of butter (or margarine) and oil is best for achieving high heat without burning. If several pieces of something—e.g., slices of meat—are to be browned, spread them out in one layer in your skillet rather than piling them one on top of the other. And when browning anything, watch it carefully to be sure that it is browned, rather than burned or cooked inside.

As a finishing touch, browning means applying heat to

achieve a delicate brown color on a topping, as on *au gratin* dishes.

Brush (with): to apply a liquid or liquid mixture by painting on with a pastry brush or by spreading over the surface of the food with a piece of wax paper or a paper towel that has been dipped in the liquid.

Canapé: a small section of bread or toast—occasionally, a cracker—covered with a tasty spread or mixture, usually planned for pleasant appearance as well as taste, and often decoratively garnished. The word implies a greater formality—as well as creative forethought—than "snacks" or plain "cheese and crackers."

Carmelize: to melt and heat sugar slowly, over low heat, until it becomes a thick golden-brown liquid; the resulting liquid is used in cake icings, candies, etc.

Casserole: a dish, usually consisting of several ingredients, prepared and served in the same container, usually cooked by baking; the container in which such a dish is prepared—a heatproof glass, earthenware, or metal pot that comes with a cover and is both ovenworthy and attractive.

Chill: to place in the refrigerator until substantially below room temperature.

Chop: to cut, with a knife or food chopper, into small pieces. It is important that your cutting implement be sharp, or you will bruise or tear rather than chop. (Also see DICE; MINCE.)

Chopping a flimsy food such as parsley can pose problems. Some cooks, despairing of keeping a knife sharp enough to do the job (and it must be very sharp), prefer to use kitchen shears. But they must be sharp too.

Clarify: to strain or otherwise deal with a liquid so as to remove solid materials and end up with something perfectly clear.

Clarifying melted butter involves patient stirring during the melting process, extremely low heat, plus occasional removal of the pan from the heat source until the thick froth disappears, then letting the butter sit until solids have precipitated to the bottom, and straining off the clear upper portion.

Coat: to cover food with a thin but consistent coating (as of flour or crumbs), usually prior to frying or baking.

Meat or poultry pieces may be coated with flour by rolling them in the flour or by sprinkling flour over the food or, more easily, by putting the flour (along with specified seasonings) and the food in a plastic or paper bag, holding the mouth of the bag tightly closed, and shaking vigorously.

Confectioners' Sugar: a finely pulverized form of sugar, used for such purposes as cake frostings; to be used only when so specified in a recipe, and not exchangeable with ordinary (granulated) sugar.

Consommé: a clear soup, not containing any solid food pieces, usually made from beef or poultry in combination with other flavorings.

Cream: to work a solid fat such as butter until it acquires a soft, creamy consistency; a recipe will often direct that this be done in combination with another ingredient, such as sugar. Best way: put the fat in a bowl, do the creaming with the back of a wooden spoon; it will go faster if the bowl is first rinsed out with boiling water, thus speeding the softening process.

Creaming is a handy way to incorporate special flavorings, typically for use as a canapé spread—as, anchovies. Cream the butter alone first, then cream in the flavorings, and refrigerate the mixture until you're ready to serve.

Croutons: small cubes of fried or toasted bread, sprinkled as a garnish on dishes such as soups.

Cut and Fold: same as FOLD.

Cut In: to work solid shortening—e.g., butter—into flour or other dry mixture until the fat is in very small pieces evenly distributed throughout the mixture; may be done with the fingers, but more efficiently performed with two knives or with a pastry blender.

Dash: less than one-quarter of a teaspoonful; usually applied to spices or seasonings.

Deep-Fry: to fry in a saucepan or kettle, deep enough to float or immerse the food being fried.

Deglaze: to pour liquid into a pan in which meat has been cooked—after removing the meat and degreasing the pan—and, as the liquid simmers, to scrape up coagulated drippings into the liquid, thus rescuing otherwise lost meat flavors; such a liquid then serves as a base for sauce or gravy to be served with the meat.

Degrease: to remove excess fat from the surface of a liquid, either during cooking, or after cooking (or a stage in the cooking) has been completed. If the liquid has completely cooled, there's no problem; the fat (as in a meat stock you may wish to keep and use at another time) will have congealed solidly on top, and can simply be lifted off in chunks.

If the liquid is cooking or still hot, there are a number of methods that can be used. One—especially if it's not necessary to remove every bit of the fat—is simply spooning it off. Another—useful if the food has been removed from the pan—is to use paper towels to blot the grease from the surface. A third is to draw off the fat with a baster. And still another, most useful with a partially cooled liquid, is to use one or more ice cubes; drawn across the surface, they will chill it just enough for the fat to congeal on the cube.

Dice: to cut into small cube-shaped pieces.

Divide: to separate a given ingredient into two equal parts (unless another number is specified), to be used at two different stages in a recipe.

Dot: to place small pieces of an ingredient (as, butter) at random intervals over the surface of a prepared dish, usually prior to cooking it.

Drain: to remove as much liquid as possible, by spreading on paper toweling, for example (as, lettuce leaves), or by pouring into a sieve or colander and letting the liquid run through (as, canned fruit, or vegetables, or cooked pasta).

Draw: to cut open a fowl or fish and remove the entrails; also, to steep (as, tea) in order to coax out all flavor.

Dredge: to coat thoroughly by dipping into the specified substance, usually flour (or a mixture of flour and seasonings), crumbs, or sugar.

Dress: to remove the feathers from poultry; sometimes, to remove the head, feet, and/or entrails as well. (See Chapter III for a detailed discussion of this and other poultry-selling terms.)

Drippings: fats and juices left in the pan after meat has been roasted, broiled, browned, or fried.

Enriched: describing white bread or flour to which vitamins and minerals have been added to make it more nearly equal in food value to natural whole wheat.

Escallop: same as SCALLOP.

Fillet: a slice of boneless meat or fish; to remove the bone and cut into such slices.

Flake: to break into small pieces with a fork (as, canned fish).

Flambé: to flame a dish immediately prior to serving it, by pouring liqueur, brandy, or other alcoholic substance over it, then igniting the liquid; describing a dish so served.

Be sure to warm your liqueur or other spirits slightly first; if it's cold it will be difficult, if not impossible, to ignite.

Fold: to combine two ingredients or mixtures, one of which has usually been whipped, so as to retain as much of the airiness as possible. The procedure is to place the whipped substance on top of the other in the bowl, then to mix them by cutting down through both ingredients, coming across the bottom and up the side, and folding some of the bottom ingredient over the top; this cutting-down-and-folding-up-the-side motion is repeated until the two substances have been mixed. A spoon may be used for folding, but a rubber spatula is far better.

French: to trim meat away from the end of a bone, e.g., from a rib lamp chop; also, to cut green beans into lengthwise strips, removing and discarding the seeds.

French-Fry: same as DEEP-FRY.

Fricassee: to braise meat or poultry that has been cut into serving pieces, adding a little water, broth, or sauce at the second stage; a dish so prepared.

Frost: to add a topping or allover coating of icing to cake or other pastry.

Fry: to cook in fat or oil, uncovered, without any other liquid.

If you have splattering trouble when frying, try sprinkling some salt in the skillet before putting in the fat or oil.

Sunny-side-up eggs tend to get overcooked and crackly on the underside, while the area around the yolk remains undone. Prevent this by covering the pan or skillet as soon as most of the white is fairly well set (if you haven't a lid,

make a dome of aluminum foil); the cover will reflect the heat back and speed setting of the top surface (peek frequently to see if it's done).

Calorie counters will be better off avoiding frying—cooking meats, fish, and poultry instead by such greaseless methods as baking or broiling.

Garnish: to decorate with something edible but not an integral part of the dish—as, croutons in soup, or parsley on almost anything; the food so used.

Glaze: to apply a shiny coating to a food, whether or not during cooking—a sugar glaze on baked ham, for example, or a butter-and-brown-sugar glaze on braised carrots.

Breads or cookies may be softly glazed by brushing on a bit of beaten egg white about ten minutes before baking is completed.

Grate: to shred in small bits by rubbing over a grater or (for foods that are in, or can be cut into, small pieces) by using a rotary grater or a blender. The latter methods are far easier, and also permit less fingering of the food, hence less flavor loss.

Gravy: a sauce made by combining meat drippings with seasonings and, often, a thickening agent such as flour or cornstarch.

Grease: to rub a pan, casserole, baking dish, or other cooking utensil with fat or oil to prevent the food from sticking during heating.

Grill: same as BROIL, but often used, now, to refer specifically to outdoor cooking on patio or picnic ground.

Grind: to shred food into exceedingly small bits by putting it through a mechanical grinder or chopper; usually used only in reference to meats.

Ice: same as FROST; also, to chill by adding ice.

Julienne: to cut into matchstick-slim strips, usually (though not always) applied to vegetables such as carrots or potatoes; describing a dish so prepared.

Knead: to manipulate dough with the hands until it is smooth and pliable. A simple and effective method for bread or other dough is to turn it out on a lightly floured board; then fold the dough toward you, press down and away with the heel of your hand, give the dough a quarter-turn, and repeat the same three steps, continuing until the dough is smooth and elastic and no longer sticks to the board.

Lard: to place strips of bacon, fat, or salt pork on meat so that they melt onto, and baste, the meat during cooking; or, to insert such strips into the meat with a larding needle, for the same purpose.

Leaven: to raise—as, dough; leavening agents such as baking powder or yeast are usually incorporated in baking. (Also see QUICK BREAD.)

Liquor: the liquid in which a food, such as canned fruit, is packed. (Also see POT LIQUOR.)

Lukewarm: a temperature that feels slightly warm, but not hot, to the hand—generally defined as about 100°-110° F.

Macerate: same as MARINATE, but usually used only to refer to fruits.

Marinate: to let stand in a liquid, prior to cooking, to impart a special flavor and sometimes to tenderize as well. Such a liquid, called a marinade, may contain a variety of ingredients or types of ingredients; oil, vinegar, wine, lemon juice, herbs, and spices are among them.

Melt: to liquefy by applying heat. When melting chocolate for frosting, use a double boiler, and melt the chocolate over simmering, rather than boiling, water (steam from the boiling water will overmoisten the chocolate and adversely affect the drying time of the frosting).

Meringue: a stiffly beaten mixture of egg whites and sugar, usually—though not necessarily—baked, e.g., as topping for a pie.

Mince: to chop into superfine pieces.

Mousse: a molded dish containing gelatin and cream; sometimes a dessert dish (containing fruit or other flavoring, and usually frozen); sometimes a baked or steamed main dish including meat, fish, and/or vegetables.

Pan-Broil: to cook on top of the range, in a pan or skillet, with no fat or with just the barest amount of fat necessary to prevent sticking. As in broiling, be sure to slash surrounding fat at intervals to prevent curling.

Pan-Fry: variously used to mean the same as FRY or SAUTÉ—and occasionally used when PAN-BROIL is intended. A confusing term, and one probably best eliminated.

Pan Gravy: a gravy made without added thickeners. To make pan gravy, the meat juices and drippings in the roasting or frying pan are simmered (perhaps with the addition of a little water) to dissolve solid residues, then boiled down; additional touches, such as chestnuts or mushrooms, may then be added and briefly simmered in the liquid.

Parboil: to cook in boiling water to a point short of doneness, often because the cooking is to be completed in some other manner or in combination with other ingredients. The time may vary, depending on the purpose, from something barely beyond blanching to a period nearly but not quite sufficient to complete cooking (as, for example, when the ingredient is to be blended with several others in a casserole, and the brief period of less intense cooking there will be sufficient to complete cooking).

Pare: to remove the outer skin or peel from a fruit or vegetable. In paring vegetables, pare as thinly as possible; many essential vitamins and minerals lurk very close to the surface. A simple, easy-to-use paring device is generally available, and does a far better job than a knife on such things as potatoes and carrots.

Pinch: a scant one-eighth of a teaspoon, presumably the amount of a seasoning one can pinch between one's thumb and index finger (Also see DASH).

Pit: to remove the pit or seeds of a fruit.

Poach: to cook in liquid below the boiling point, at the simmer or just below.

Fish should be poached at a trembling, rather than a simmering, point, to prevent disintegration.

To keep poaching eggs from separating, add a drop of lemon juice or vinegar to the water; it won't change the taste.

Pot Liquor: the liquid in which a vegetable or vegetables have been cooked (usually, boiled); save it for reheating the leftovers or for incorporating in other dishes such as stews.

Pot Roast: to cook a large piece of meat by braising, specifically on top of the range; a cut of meat appropriate for cooking in such a manner, but also capable of being roasted or baked, if done in such a way as to hold in the juices (as, by totally enclosing in foil, together with seasonings).

Preheat: to bring an oven to cooking temperature prior to inserting the food to be cooked. Familiarity with your oven is a valuable culinary plus; whatever preheating time recipes may specify, ovens vary considerably in time required, and it's well to be acquainted with the peculiarities and proclivities of your own appliances.

Purée: to put an ingredient, or a combination of ingredients, through a sieve, blender, strainer, food mill, or other device, so that the result is a pulpy but flowing mass; also, the result of such a procedure.

Quick Bread: bread made by using baking powder or soda, rather than yeast, as the leavening agent; such bread is faster to make, but cannot be kept as long. The term also includes biscuits, muffins, etc., made in this manner.

In baking any sort of quick breads, the double-action type of baking powder is preferred to the tartrate and phosphate types. The former is designed to go to work in the presence of oven heat, rather than before; it may therefore be sifted into the baking mixture right along with other dry ingredients, and the quick bread will not be harmed if there is some delay in getting the batter or dough into the oven.

Ramekin: a small casserole designed to hold one serving.

Reconstitute: to restore a concentrate, whether frozen or simply dehydrated, to its original state, usually by adding water.

Reduce: to diminish in volume (and simultaneously concentrate flavor, enrich, and thicken) by boiling.

Rehydrate: to restore previously removed water content.

Render: to heat a solid fat to the melting point, usually so that it can be easily removed, whether for discard or for storage and later use.

Reserve: to keep for later use, as in (referring to a canned fruit) "drain, reserve syrup"—meaning that the ingredient in question should be drained not down the drain, but into a bowl or other container.

Rice: to press through a ricer or coarse sieve; a step in preparing mashed potatoes and other dishes.

Roast: to cook by dry heat, as in an oven (see BAKE).

In roasting large cuts of meat, such as beef or leg of lamb, it is generally a good idea to start the oven at a slightly higher temperature, then reduce it to the regular roasting temperature after ten or fifteen minutes (for a further discussion of cooking temperatures, see Chapter VIII). Let a roast sit for five to fifteen minutes after removing it from the oven, before slicing. Both these steps help to hold in the essential juices.

Roll Out: to flatten out dough with a rolling pin so that it may be cut into the desired size and shape for pie crust or cookies.

Pastry dough will roll out more easily and smoothly if it is wrapped in wax paper and refrigerated for about half an hour before rolling. Roll it out on a board lightly dusted with flour to prevent sticking (if it sticks during rolling, add a little more flour), always rolling from the center outward, and turning the dough at intervals (which also helps to prevent sticking).

Roux: a blend of melted fat (usually butter) and flour, cooked together briefly to form the basis of a thick sauce or gravy.

Good basic proportions for the two ingredients are two tablespoons of butter for each three tablespoons of flour. The butter is melted first over low heat; the flour is then stirred in and the blend cooked slowly, with continuous stirring, for two to five minutes before other liquid is added.

If you are making a white sauce, use an enameled or copper saucepan rather than steel or aluminum, as the latter can discolor the sauce.

Salted Water: opinions vary as to precisely what ratio of salt to water is intended by this ubiquitous recipe instruction, and experienced cooks don't worry about it. If you feel more secure measuring, a safe standard is one to two teaspoonfuls of salt to each quart of water.

Sauté: to cook in a very small quantity of very hot fat or oil, with or without the addition of seasonings, sometimes as a preliminary to other cooking, sometimes to cook the food completely.

The general guidelines for browning apply here—the fat heated before the food is put in, the food as dry as possible, and so on. If the food to be sautéed is to be dredged in flour, do so immediately before cooking it; otherwise, the juices are likely to seep through the flour coating and be lost.

Scald: to heat to a point just short of boiling, removing the pan from the heat source the moment that point is reached.

Scallop: a slice of veal—rarely, other meats as well—cut about half an inch thick, then pounded to a thickness of a quarter of an inch or less. Also, to cook such meat slices, or any food, with a topping of crumbs or crumbs-and-cheese and sauce.

Score: to make gashes with a knife without cutting entirely through; ham, for example, is often scored in a crisscross pattern before baking.

Sear: to brown the surface of meat or poultry quickly at high temperature, either on top of the stove or in the oven, during the first few minutes of cooking.

Always sear before salting the meat; salt will simply draw out the juices you're trying to seal in.

Season: to add salt, pepper, and other flavorings, such as herbs or spices.

Separate: to divide an egg or eggs so that the yolk and white may be handled differently or incorporated in the dish at different stages, or in order to use only the one or the other in the particular dish.

Eggs are most easily separated when cold, so keep them in the refrigerator until you're ready to proceed.

For separating, have two small bowls or other containers ready. Crack the egg, then hold the two halves just slightly apart to let most of the white run out. Open the egg and juggle the yolk back and forth between the two halves until you have collected all the white completely, then slide the yolk into your second bowl.

If the acrobatics of all this prove too much, another way is to set a small funnel over a narrow glass and spill the egg's entire contents in; the funnel will catch the yolk, while the white will slip through into the glass.

Shortening: fat or oil. If a recipe specifies "melted shortening," and the taste of butter isn't essential, it's easiest to simply measure out the required amount of bottled oil.

Shred: to tear into narrow strips, either by hand (as, lettuce) or by grating.

Sift: to put flour, or flour in combination with other dry ingredients, through a sifter, a mechanical device that shakes the flour through a series of fine sieves.

Flour should be measured after sifting, not before. The easiest way to accomplish the job is to place your measuring cup on a large piece of wax paper, and sift into the cup (the excess then falls onto the paper). Level off your measure, and retrieve the extra sifted flour by just picking up the wax paper and pouring it back into your flour bin.

Simmer: to cook gently, over very low heat, in liquid kept just below the boiling point (at sea level, about 185°-205°F.). The bubbles should form slowly, most breaking beneath the surface of the liquid, only an occasional one rising to the top.

Singe: to turn a chicken or other fowl rapidly over a flame to burn off feather wisps or hairs.

Skewer: a long pin of wood or metal, usually the latter; to use such a pin to hold meat or poultry together while cooking; also, to use such a pin, in longer form, to hold small pieces of meat and vegetables cooked over fire or grill.

Skim: to remove fat or other material from the surface of a liquid. (Also see DEGREASE.)

Slice: to cut across into segments. Slicing a round, wobbly item such as an onion or potato is made easier by first cutting a thin slice off one side to make a flat, steady surface.

Soft Ball Stage: a temperature point in candy-making (see Chapter VIII).

Soufflé: a type of baked dish—which may contain a variety of ingredients and appear as a main course or as a dessert, depending on content and flavoring—made especially light, airy, and high-rising by the incorporation of separately beaten egg whites.

Steam: to cook in steam by placing the food, in a covered container, above boiling water. May be done in a specially designed utensil called a steamer, or in a pressure cooker, or by improvising in a kettle; the important thing, in the latter case, is to be sure that the food is definitely above the surface of the boiling water.

Steep: to let stand for a time in hot liquid in order to extract full flavor—as, from tea leaves.

Stew: to cook slowly, in a covered pot or kettle, with just enough liquid to cover the food being cooked; also, the dish thus prepared, usually a combination of meat or poultry (cut in near-bite-size or serving pieces) and vegetables.

Long cooking over low heat, with the liquid kept at a simmer, favors the mingling and thorough blending of flavors that is the essence of a successful stew. Many people, including the author's husband, find the flavor of stew improved—drawn out and intensified—upon reheating of the leftover portion.

Stews may be almost infinitely varied from one making to another, even if based upon the same recipe, by the inclusion of different herbs and seasonings, the substitution or addition of other vegetables, or the use of a different base for the liquid (condensed soups, such as tomato, work well).

Stir: to agitate with a spoon or fork, in a circular motion, in order to blend ingredients, or to keep a substance in motion to prevent burning or sticking while cooking.

Stir rice with fork, never with spoon, which tends to lump the grains together.

Stock: the liquid in which meat, poultry, or fish has been cooked; rarely used in reference to vegetables. Stock, like pot liquor, is a good thing to save in a covered jar in the refrigerator; it can be used to enhance and vary the flavor of almost anything requiring liquid for cooking—stews, soups, and so on. Stock (degreased, of course) can in fact be substituted for water in boiling foods such as vegetables or rice, if the flavor is suitable.

Toast: to brown by direct heat, as under a broiler, on a grill, or in an electric toaster; bread so browned.

Toss: to mix a combination of solid ingredients—as, in a salad—by repeated lifting with a fork or with a fork and spoon.

Truss: to tie poultry with twine, or a combination of skewers and twine, so that stuffing will not spill out and legs and wings will remain in position during roasting.

Whip: to beat a liquid—e.g., egg whites or whipping cream—until it has increased substantially in volume and become fluffy and light.

Whipping cream will whip up more successfully if you've prechilled both bowl and whip. Be sure, too, that anything to which you must add the whipped cream is also cold; otherwise, the cream will tend to liquefy and deflate. Bear in mind, incidentally, that cream doubles in volume when whipped, and recipe phrasing must be carefully noted; "one cup of cream, whipped" denotes twice as much as "one cup of whipped cream."

XXXX Sugar: same as CONFECTIONERS' SUGAR.

III.   Guide to Shrewd Shopping:
General Marketing, Packaged Foods, Meats, Poultry, Fish, and Dairy Items

Clever marketing for your family's food needs results from a combination of factors—adding up, in the end, to truly wise use of your budget. Which does not necessarily mean buying what is the lowest in price, since what you get for your money, whether you spend a little or a lot, is the prime factor. Your food dollar buys quantity—box, bottle, or pound—of course; but it also buys, depending on your needs and desires, superior taste, nutrition, health protection, convenience of preparation, services.

Label-reading and noting of price tags is a fairly obvious must; be sure, first of all, that you are charged the proper price for the quantity you buy. Be certain that the scales in your grocery or supermarket are accurate, and that prepackaged meats and vegetables contain the labeled weight. Be aware of measures generally: know that a "huge half-quart" is nothing more than a pint, for instance, and compare costs with other mere pints of the same sort of product. (See Chapter VII for all the important weight-and-measure data.) You may need to do a little calculating, but the law does require that contents and price be plainly stated (and if usage of the product requires the addition of other foods, that's part of the cost, too, and must be figured in). If you find a price misstated, or a product—whether packaged or fresh—short-weighted, don't hesitate to report it: first to the store owner or manager (mistakes do happen), then, if there's no satisfaction forthcoming, to local or state authorities.

Labels should, incidentally, be taken quite literally, so far as product descriptions go. "Orange drink" means exactly what it says; it does not mean orange juice, and is unlikely to taste like—or have other qualities of—the juice. The government, happily, is fairly strict about these things; but manufacturers are fairly bright about dreaming up enticing phrasing, too. Another handy thing to know is that in mixture products—a canned stew, for example—ingredients must be listed in order of their proportions; "beef stew" that—in the small print—lists potatoes first is not apt to be especially beefy.

Most of this chapter and the next one will be concerned with the matter of quality, with guidelines for judging the worth of what you buy, regardless of price, especially in the fresh-foods area. A word, though, about the matter of money; other things (such as cleanliness and freshness) being equal, there are a few penny-saving ploys of which the shrewd shopper should be aware. Though, as noted below, it pays in the long run to patronize stores regularly, it also pays to watch for locally advertised special offers; check them out personally, of course—and if they turn out to be truly good values, take advantage of them (fine meat, for example, may be extra-low-priced at a particular market one week, and it will pay to buy then, freeze for later use). Start your shopping, in any case, with a list; avoid impulse buying, especially of non-storable items (when you buy regularly at one market, incidentally, you can save many minutes of aisle-trudging by making your list follow store layout).

Bear in mind, as you budget, that these four rules hold generally true: First, stores that give trading stamps often boost prices. Second, store brands—with no money devoted to costly promotion—are frequently top quality and cost far less than nationally advertised names. Third, it costs a company more to package a quantity (as, of cereal) in many small boxes than in one large box—and you'll pay more, too. Fourth, prepared foods—precooked, frozen, heat-and-serve, "instant" mixes—charge you for the work involved as well as for the food itself; if time's worth money to you, then pay for the convenience—but if not, it's worth mashing your own potatoes, baking your own biscuits, and the like.

If you've just moved into a neighborhood, spend some time shopping around, getting acquainted with both personnel and merchandise at local markets. Then, settle if you can for a regular grocer, butcher, and so on, on whom you know you can rely, and who will in turn give you the special service reserved for regular patrons. It's the lady who returns week after week, representing continued income for the store, who'll really get the choice cuts of meat, the freshest eggs, the best selection when she phones in a grocery order.

Fresh foods—meats, poultry, fish, dairy items, fruits and vegetables—offer the greatest challenge to the shopper, and we'll spell out detailed criteria for them; meats, poultry, fish, and dairy items are covered in this chapter, fruits and vegetables in Chapter IV. But first, a brief comment on

PACKAGED FOODS

Frozen and canned foods are pretty well regulated, therefore pretty dependable; the government is quick to seize huge shipments if the slightest danger or irregularity is even suspected. Canned food, in particular, can be completely trusted, since no harm can befall it (assuming the can is undamaged) between the grower or packer and you. There are Federal grades for canned food as for fresh, though packers aren't required to spell them out, and most don't. You may occasionally find fruits or vegetables or other items marked "Grade A" or "Fancy" (both mean the same thing), and that's a definite claim that the food is prime quality in color, shape, flavor, and uniform size of the items inside (as, slices of pineapple); absence of the grade doesn't imply inferior quality, though.

Frozen foods, however, are a slightly different story. Here, a great deal depends on the handling of the package between packer and store, and in the store itself. Maintenance of quality means the package must be kept solidly frozen. Some stores overstack their frozen food bins, and topmost items end up above the safe-temperature line; make a habit of reaching underneath. If the package is soft in any case, start buying your frozen foods elsewhere. A lumpy package? Don't blame the grocer for this one. If the solid material seems to have collected at one end, it's evidence that somewhere in prior handling, the package was thawed and refrozen—with inevitable deterioration in the quality of its contents; pick another package.

One other kind of packaged food, baked goods, may present a quality problem, usually resulting from careless store management. Bread—of whatever type—should be securely wrapped and (except for the hard crusts of rye or pumpernickel) feel soft and yielding if it's fresh. If the wrapper's transparent, check to be sure there are no signs of mold. In sweet items—pies, cakes, doughnuts, and so on—be sure there are no insects or other crawly things. There's not likely to be a baked-goods problem where the manager or owner runs a clean shop and keeps an eye on the freshness of his merchandise.

MEATS

Meat shipped in interstate commerce must be inspected; some, at the packer's option, is Federally graded as well (all graded meat has been inspected, but the reverse is not necessarily true).

In the absence of grading, your clue to wholesomeness—at least when the meat left the packing plant—is the round purple stamp (the dye is harmless) that says "U.S. INSPECTED." Such meat, whatever its cut or quality in terms of taste, is safe, untainted, free of disease. (The store must, of course, keep all meat under refrigeration, whether in display case or "cold room," and the meat should look and smell fresh.)

Beef is the meat most often graded; lamb and veal are occasionally graded; pork is not graded by the Federal government, though state or local authorities may establish local criteria. And remember that grading isn't required; ungraded meat may still be of superior quality.

Grades appear in the form of a shield-shaped purple stamp bearing the letters "USDA" (for United States Department of Agriculture) and the name of the grade. The five official grades and their significance, in descending order:

USDA PRIME—excellent quality; tender and juicy; good distribution (marbling) of fat through the lean meat; fat covering thick, and white to creamy in color.

USDA CHOICE—very good quality; quite tender; moderate fat distribution; fat covering a bit thinner, perhaps slightly yellowed. This is the top grade carried by the average butcher who carries graded meat.

USDA GOOD—good quality; relatively tender; a high ratio of lean to fat, with little or no marbling; fat covering fairly thin and yellow.

USDA STANDARD—markedly less tender, with a high proportion of lean meat and a very thin fat covering; but from an animal still under the age of four years.

USDA COMMERCIAL—apt to lack tenderness; predominantly from older animals; a definite lack of fat.

Whether or not you choose high-grade meat should depend at least in part on how you plan to use it. For broiling or roasting, where the flavor and texture of the meat are of the essence, your best choice is one of the top three grades, and the better you can afford, the tastier your steak or roast. For other uses, where long, moist cooking is involved, and where the meat may be combined with other ingredients, a lower, more economical grade may be satisfactory; GOOD, STANDARD, or even COMMERCIAL meat may be fine for stewing or braising, or for use in hamburger or meat loaf.

Lower grades are just as nutritious as higher ones, of course. In fact, they actually give you more meat for your money, since there is less fat—which contributes to flavor and tenderness far more than to nutritive value.

Do make a point of purchasing meat from a market or butcher store where you are permitted to examine the merchandise from all sides. There's no telling what lurks on the underside of a prepackaged steak or chop displayed in a plastic-covered cardboard tray; prepackaging is fine (though not, as noted below, for ground meats), but the container should be fully transparent.

One further note on butchers. They are generally very helpful, whether you are a beginner or an experienced cook. A reliable butcher can be the cook's best friend. He can explain cuts to you (don't be afraid to ask—he's the expert, you're not expected to be). He can suggest more economical cuts for your purpose. He can advise on the best buys for your cooking needs—and often can give you valuable pointers on the preparation itself. Make friends with your butcher, and you, your family, and your dinner guests will reap the rewards.

Beef: This is the meat most commonly Federally graded, and those grades are a good guide to follow. Top-grade beef is light red, with a velvety look, and well marbled with fat; the bones are reddish, and the fat quite light in color.

Beef cuts, like grades, should be chosen for your cooking use, for some are more expensive than others (and prices can vary considerably, even within the same store, based on supply and demand); here again, the best cuts— prime rib roast, porterhouse, sirloin, T-bone, and such— are best reserved for roasting and broiling. The lowest-cost cuts—shank or neck, for example—are fine (especially if they are at least of GOOD grade) for stew and for braised dishes like pot roast. Even for these, of course, your dish will taste better if you have one of the better cuts. Among the best for stew are sirloin tip, rump, chuck, and bottom round; for pot roast, the best are sirloin tip, chuck, top, bottom, or eye round.

In any case, a lower-priced cut can usually be substituted for a higher-priced one if it is of highest grade. A CHOICE quality chuck steak may be at least as good as a lower-quality porterhouse, for example. Better markets often age high-grade meats, a process that increases tenderness and flavor; an aged steak, whatever the cut, is usually a very good bet.

Almost any cut can be used for hamburger; it's mainly a matter of personal preference. Some, including the writer, are partial to top or bottom round; others like burgers made from less expensive cuts—chuck, neck, or whatever is available. In any case, the fat should be trimmed prior to grinding, and you should see exactly what you're getting; have the meat ground before your eyes, unless you are very, very sure of your butcher.

Calves' Liver: This is the only interesting part of an animal that's too old to be veal and too young to be beef. Calves' liver is desirable because—unlike the older beef liver—it does not contain the large, tough tubing (veins) that must be removed from beef liver before it can be cooked (both have a thin membrane around the edge of the slice, but that's easily slit and peeled off). Calves' liver is also very expensive.

Beef liver costs less, is just as tasty and nutritious. And

if you are fortunate enough to have a butcher who can obtain for you something meat-business men refer to as "young beef" liver, then your worries are entirely over; since it's not classified as calf, it's far less costly—and since the animal is nevertheless a very young one, barely beyond the calf stage, you can prepare the liver just as you would calves' liver, and it will be nearly as tender.

Lamb: Lamb, like veal or calf, represents a specific early stage of an animal, and costs a bit more than the later, or sheep, stage. The younger the lamb, the higher the cost— so it's vital for the shrewd shopper to know the difference between the various ages and stages. There are four.

HOTHOUSE LAMB or MILK-FED LAMB is available only in early spring, and is considered a delicacy. The lamb is properly no more than two to three months old, and the flesh is pale whitish-pink. Hothouse lamb is excellent for broiling or roasting.

SPRING LAMB is available a little later, and comes from animals from three to four months old; the flesh is now red, but still pale. Spring lamb offers fine quality for broiling, roasting, stew.

LAMB is lamb until the animal reaches the age of one year; the meat is bright red, with firm white fat. The older the animal, the less suitable its flesh for roasting and the better for braising, fricasseeing, stewing, and such.

MUTTON comes from a sheep, not a lamb—an animal over a year old (but properly less than two years old). Mutton meat is darker in color, its fat less firm and beginning to crumble. Mutton needs long cooking, but is an acceptable stew meat, though used far less in the U.S. than in some other countries.

Leg (or half-leg) or shoulder are the cuts of choice for roast lamb; most butchers will also be happy to provide a boned-and-rolled leg or shoulder (the bone removed, the flesh rolled and securely tied or netted), which makes a very nice, compact roast. Chops—loin, rib, or shoulder, according to your preference and your purse—are good for broiling, and a double-thick chop makes a fine single-serving steak for broiling, pan-broiling, or braising. Other cuts—neck, breast, short ribs, shanks—are fine for long-cooking braised dishes and for stews; neck or shank meat is good for grinding into "lamburgers," too.

Pork: Pork is marketed both fresh and cured (the latter is called bacon or ham). Top-quality fresh pork is firm and fine-grained, varying in color from pale pink to rosy depending on the age of the animal; the fat should be very white, soft, and smooth. It's best to select cuts with little fat cover, since the meat itself is naturally heavily larded.

Leg, shoulder, and various loin cuts are good for roasting, while the chops and steaks (usually cut from the shoulder) are generally braised or sautéed. Smoked hams may be roasted, baked, or cooked on top of the stove; steaks cut from them, sautéed, baked or—more often—braised.

Bacon is of course a smoked-pork staple in American homes. If you buy the packaged kind, check it to make sure there's no mold (bacon doesn't keep as long as some people, and some stores, think it does), and get it as lean as possible to prevent shrinkage waste; the kind your butcher slices from a slab sometimes costs a little more than the packaged, but may be worth it, since shrinkage is often significantly less.

Specialty Meats: The thing to remember about all specialty meats—kidneys, liver, sweetbreads, brains, and so on—is that they are extremely perishable. Get assurance that they are fresh, and buy only what you intend to use the same day.

Veal: Veal comes, specifically, from animals three to twelve weeks old; after that, the animal is a calf, and the meat has neither the delicacy of the baby animal nor the fat development and flavor of the adult (calves' liver, though, as previously noted, is highly prized). Veal should be smooth and quite pale, ranging in color from a very light pink (for a milk-fed animal, considered most desirable) to a somewhat darker pink (if there has been any grass-feeding); there is little if any fat, and what there is has a pink-white color.

Cutlets and scallops—cut from various parts of the animal—are the most widely used of the veal cuts, with chops (loin, rib, or shoulder) a close second; they are usually cooked by some form of braising. If you are planning one of the popular Italian dishes such as Veal Scallopini or Veal Parmigiana, be sure you have the super-thin scallops (have your butcher do the pounding with his heavy mallet or the side of his cleaver).

A number of cuts—top round, sirloin, loin, leg, shoulder—make good boned-and-rolled roasts. For veal stew, choose breast, short ribs, chops, neck, shank, or rump. Almost any of the cuts, including the less expensive ones, may be ground for "vealburgers" or veal loaf.

POULTRY

Happily, current cookbooks are not likely to begin poultry recipes with "first, catch and kill your chicken." Dressed birds are now everywhere available, and the modern homemaker is spared the role of executioner. "Dressed" means, in some locales, that the bird has been bled and picked, though head, feet, and entrails may not have been removed; in other areas, though, the word is equivalent to ready-to-cook. A "ready-to-cook" bird has been dressed, and has had its head, feet, entrails, and oil sac removed as well, and its pinfeathers pulled; it has been cleaned inside and out, and the giblets (gizzard, liver, and heart) and often the neck have usually been separately wrapped and packed inside.

Ready-to-cook birds may also be inspected and officially quality-graded. Poultry identified as Federally inspected (usually on a hang-tag attached to wing or leg) has been processed under government supervision and inspected and passed as wholesome. Additionally, some poultry has been graded under Federal or Federal-state auspices and may then carry a shield-shaped grade mark classing it as U.S. GRADE A, U.S. GRADE B, or U.S. GRADE C; these grades denote overall quality based on the bird's general conformation, freedom from feathers, and absence of injury or other blemishes.

For highest quality, choose a well-fleshed bird; fat should be especially generously distributed over breast and legs. The skin should be creamy to yellow, relatively unblemished, and certainly not torn. Discolorations, sliminess, and odd odors are all clues to possible spoilage; check the area beneath the wings, in particular.

Chickens: Most chickens, these days, are sold ready-to-cook and chilled, and may be bought whole, cut in half, or cut up in serving pieces for frying, broiling, or stewing. Many markets also sell specific parts by the pound to suit individual preferences—legs, thighs, wings, or breasts.

Chickens are classified according to age and sex, each type offering different advantages, depending on intended use and prevailing prices. Terms in general use are:

BROILER—chicken of either sex, from seven to twelve weeks old and weighing from 1 to 2½ pounds; very young and tender, fine for either broiling or frying.

FRYER—male from fourteen to twenty weeks old, weighing from 2 to 3½ pounds; also young and tender, and good for either broiling or frying. Large fryers are suitable for roasting as well.

ROASTER—male from five to nine months old and weighing over 3½ pounds—a still-young bird, still tender, and full-flavored; for roasting, and also for frying, fricasseeing, and use in casserole dishes.

CAPON—desexed male from seven to ten months old, upwards of 4 pounds in weight, and better-fleshed than a roaster; good for the same cooking uses.

PULLET or YOUNG HEN—female from four to nine months old, weighing from 2½ to 5½ pounds; a still-tender bird good for frying, roasting, fricasseeing, or stewing.

STEWING CHICKEN or HEN—female of a somewhat more advanced age, from ten to twelve months, though weighing about the same as a younger hen; best for long-cooking dishes such as stews and fricassees.

FOWL or OLD HEN—female more than a year old, less tender but still usable for such dishes as stews; weight may range upward of 2½ pounds.

COCK or ROOSTER—male at least a year old, weighing usually from 3 to 6 pounds, and quite tough; used chiefly for soup-making.

Ducks: Most ducks are marketed young (and may be called "ducklings"), under the age of six months; an older bird is really past its culinary prime. The usual weight range is from 3 to 5½ pounds; ducks are primarily roasted, but the smaller ones may also be broiled or fried.

Geese: Geese are generally marketed as "young" or "mature"; the former is by far the better buy, and for best taste and tenderness should be no more than six months old. They vary in weight from 4 to 14 pounds, though the 8-to-12-pound range is most widely available. Quite small geese may be cut in pieces for successful use in braised dishes, while the larger ones are better for roasting (geese weighing over 11 pounds may tend to be a bit tough, however).

Turkeys: Since turkey eating tends to be seasonal, more and more turkeys are now made ready-to-cook, then frozen whole and packaged in plastic bags for sale. Like chickens, they are classified—partly according to weight, partly by age. The common marketing terms:

FRYER or ROASTER—a young bird with delicate flavor. Only the smaller ones in this category, weighing 4 or 5 pounds, are fine for frying or broiling as well as for roasting; those over 5 pounds (up to about 8) should be roasted.

YOUNG TURKEY (or YOUNG HEN or YOUNG TOM)—a still-tender bird, but now with more fully developed flavor; the weight range is from 6 to 24 pounds. Hens are meatier than toms in proportion to their weight, but they seldom weigh more than 15 pounds; if you prefer a hen, and are serving a large crowd, buy two. For small-family needs, half-bird and quarter-bird roasts are sometimes available.

YEARLING—a bird no longer young, and likely to be less tender, but still possibly roastable, and certainly fine for stewing.

If none of the above terms is used, assume the turkey is definitely of advanced age and suitable only for stewing.

FISH

Unless you're sure you're going to use fresh fish the very same day (or freeze it as soon as you get it home), don't buy it; it won't keep till the next day, and you won't be happy with the state of the other foods in your fridge, once the fish has gone bad.

Naturally, even for same-day use, it's vital to be sure the fish is fresh when you buy it. Signs of same: eyes that are bright, clear, and bulging; reddish-pink gills with no slimy look to them; tightly clinging, shiny scales; firm, elastic flesh that springs back readily when you poke it; a fresh odor. If you live near a coast or inland waterway, it's helpful to know the seasons for various catches; that way, you can plan your purchasing to coincide.

Fresh fish are generally marketed in these six forms:

WHOLE or ROUND—as it suggests, the entire fish, as caught, complete with head, tail, scales, fins, and internal organs. All or most of these will have to be removed before cooking, and it's a messy job; once the fish is purchased, though, you may be able to have the dealer do the dirty work.

DRAWN—just as above, except that the entrails have been removed. Buying the fish whole or drawn has an advantage: you can check for freshness, since all the visible criteria are intact. If you feel you can trust your fish dealer, though, it's easier to buy the fish in one of the forms that follow.

DRESSED or CLEANED or PAN-DRESSED—both internal organs and scales have been removed—and, depending on the size of the fish, often the head, tail, fins, and backbone as well; some small fish, brook trout for example, are generally cooked complete with head, tail, and fins. The fish is, in any case, ready to cook.

STEAKS—cross sections of the larger dressed fish, about ½-inch to 1-inch thick, ready for cooking; each steak usually includes a cross section of the backbone.

FILLETS—the sides of the dressed fish cut lengthwise—whole fillets if the fish is fairly small, sometimes parts of fillets for a larger fish; size and weight will, of course, vary from fish to fish. Since the only bone in any fish is the backbone with its vertical extensions, fillets will be boneless or virtually so. Fillets may or may not be skinned (the skin will be only on one side, of course).

STICKS—pieces cut from fillets, usually after freezing; by general understanding, each stick weighs about an ounce and measures approximately ½ inch by ⅜ inch by 3 inches.

Many kinds of fish are available in U.S. salt and fresh waters; most are suitable for a number of cooking methods: boiling, broiling, frying, steaming, baking. You're wise to ask your trusted dealer to recommend from his fresh stock an appropriate type for the cooking method you plan to use.

SHELLFISH

The term "shellfish" actually covers two totally different—and quite unrelated—types of animals: mollusks, which include the "seashell" animals such as clams, mussels, oysters, and scallops; and crustaceans, which have jointed legs—though their skeletons are external—and include crabs, lobsters, and shrimp. Many of both categories are sold alive; all except scallops and shrimp, in fact, usually are. You can tell that a crustacean is alive if it's moving; a live bivalve mollusk holds its shell tightly closed.

Clams: As noted above, be sure that you are buying live clams; the shells should be held tightly closed (this is accomplished by a muscle, which relaxes as soon as death occurs). The principal types of clams available are:

HARD-SHELLS or QUAHOGS, also called "Little Necks" or "Cherrystones," good served raw as appetizers, also baked, and much used in soups and sauces. These clams have heavy, roughly triangular but graceful shells.

SOFT-SHELLS or STEAMERS, specifically sold for steaming and eating dipped in melted butter; this type of clam is readily identified by its long black neck, its irregularly oval shell with a small spoon-shaped projection at the hinge of one valve.

RAZOR CLAMS, used mainly for chowder-making; these clams, as their name suggests, have elongated shells shaped like straight razors.

Crabs: Crabs are marketed both alive and cooked; bear in mind that if they're alive, you must keep them that way, in wet seaweed, until cooking time (they're then killed by boiling or steaming). Both Atlantic and Pacific species are sold, the latter generally a little larger.

Hard-shell and soft-shell crabs are not different kinds, but different stages of the very same crabs. Crabs shed their shells periodically as they grow, then develop new ones; soft-shell crabs are harvested in the interim period before the new shell has properly hardened, and the shell is edible. Hard-shells are available in most areas all year round, soft-shells chiefly from late spring to mid-fall.

Lobsters: Lobsters are sold both alive and cooked, and if the latter, be sure they have been freshly cooked; if you buy a live lobster, plan to cook it without any delay. A live lobster's shell is dark green; the familiar red hue appears only after the lobster is cooked. The best quality and flavor is offered by lobsters weighing 2 pounds or slightly less, and heavy for their size; whether you purchase a male or a female depends on your personal preference (the female offers the added delicacy of "coral," the orange-colored roe, and many lobster aficionados prefer the flavor of the female; the male, on the other hand, has somewhat firmer flesh).

Two types of lobsters are commonly available on the

American market: the North Atlantic (which has large claws—and if you buy a live lobster, the claws should be pegged for your protection), and the southern type from Florida or California (which has no claws).

Lobsters, like crabs, are killed by boiling; or, if you intend to broil the lobster, severing its spinal cord will do the trick (the dealer can point out the proper spot).

Mussels: As with clams, be sure that mussel shells are firmly closed to assure that you've purchased fresh, live animals. Check their weight, too. Extra-light shells may contain diseased or underdeveloped animals, or nothing but seaweed; extra-heavy ones may be mussel-less as well, jammed with wet sand.

Oysters: As with clams and mussels, a tightly closed shell is a good sign, if you're buying live oysters (the kind to buy if you plan to serve them raw). Oysters are also sold shelled, usually by the pint or quart; live, they generally come by the dozen. Available varieties include Blue Points (best for raw-appetizer use) and others from Long Island; Cotuits from Massachusetts; Lynnhavens from Virginia; and a number of kinds from the West Coast, especially from the Puget Sound area.

It's not necessarily true, incidentally, that the only good oysters are available in months with an "R" in their names; oysters aren't as desirable during their spawning season, which runs from May through August in some locales, but the spawning season varies from place to place. It is true, though, that oysters are quite perishable—thus less dependable during the hot summer months.

Scallops: Scallops are substantially different in structure from clams, mussels, and oysters, though they are also bivalve mollusks. They're swimmers—they accomplish this by opening and closing their shells rapidly to develop a kind of jet propulsion—and thus develop a rather strong muscle (the muscle's there, but remains unde-veloped, in other bivalves); it's this muscle that makes the meat of the scallop. This muscle is separated and sold out of the shell.

There are generally two types. The Long Island (or Bay) scallop—the part you buy—is about ¾-inch thick, and pinkish-white in color; it's available from early fall through mid-spring, and is generally considered the more tasty and sweet-flavored. The larger Deep Sea Scallop is white, about 2 inches in diameter; it's generally available year round.

Shrimp: These miniature relatives of the lobster are commonly sold with heads removed, either green (uncooked) or pinkish red (boiled), either shelled or un-shelled. It's most economical to buy them uncooked and unshelled; shelling and cleaning is fairly easy, and boiling is a snap—though the odor in your kitchen isn't the most pleasant. Shrimp are also available now in shelled, boiled, individually quick-frozen form, needing only a little extra boiling; the cost is greater, but extra work is avoided, and the result is virtually the same as if you had bought them fresh.

THE DAIRY CASE

Everything in the dairy category—milk, cream, butter, eggs, cheese, and so on—must be, above all, kept refriger-ated. Anything that isn't so stored and displayed simply shouldn't be bought.

In some stores, these may be rapid-turnover items; in others, they may not. It is a good basic rule to assume that in all stores, the fresher merchandise will be put at the back and bottom of the case—so reach back and down to make your selections. Some guidelines—and in the case of eggs, some specific quality criteria—follow.

Milk & Cream: This category also includes such products as "Half and Half" (a little richer than milk, a little less rich than cream, and a good ploy for calorie counters who take cream in their coffee), skim milk, and so on. Some communities require that such products be dated; in the author's opinion, such requirements should be universal.

If your town, city, or county does so require, be sure that you are familiar with the dating system and the way it works. In New York City, for example, such products are dated—but the date represents, at the present writing, not the date the container arrived in the store, but the latest date on which it may be sold. That date is usually about two days after its arrival—so that if a New Yorker buys a quart of milk on, say, the twenty-fifth of the month, she should look for a container that is dated the twenty-seventh; consumers unfamiliar with the system are likely to pick up the nearest container bearing the current date (in our example, the twenty-fifth), or even a prior date (which unscrupulous store managers, aware of some shoppers' ignorance of the system, will leave in the display).

Cheese: These are four basic kinds of cheese available, each including a number of types. They are, with the types most generally sold in U.S. markets:

HARD—includes Parmesan, Provolone, Romano— all of Italian origin, and all often grated for garnishing Italian dishes (Parmesan and Romano are used almost exclusively for that purpose).

SEMI-HARD—includes American Cheddar, Edam, Gjetost, Gouda, Mysost, Swiss.

SEMI-SOFT—includes Blue (spelled Bleu if it is imported), Brick, Gorgonzola, Gruyère, Limburger, Muenster, Roquefort, Stilton.

SOFT—includes Bel Paese, Brie, Camembert, Cottage, Cream, Neufchâtel.

Additionally, some cheeses—cheddar, for example—are available in various flavor strengths: mild, sharp, and so on.

A number of cheeses are sold in two forms, natural and processed. Natural cheeses are carefully aged, are usually more expensive, and offer superior flavor. Processed cheeses are a blend of the natural cheese with milk or another liquid to make the finished product; though they are generally of acceptable quality and have the characteristic taste of the particular type of cheese, their flavors are somewhat "diluted."

Economically speaking, it is often worthwhile to buy cheeses unsliced and slice (or grate) your own. Little trouble is involved in the slicing or grating, you save the money paid for the manufacturer's doing it, and because you are invariably then buying from bulk natural cheeses, the flavor is often better.

Eggs: Highest-quality eggs are sold in cartons, and are graded (neither the color of the shell, nor the egg's size, incidentally, has anything to do with its quality). There are Federal, state, and private grades, applying to both size and overall quality; Federally graded eggs carry a shield-shaped grade mark on the carton. Some eggs are also dated (privately, not governmentally).

The Federal size grades most widely used, based upon weight per dozen eggs, are:

> *U.S. EXTRA LARGE*—at least 27 ounces.
> *U.S. LARGE*—at least 24 ounces.
> *U.S. MEDIUM*—at least 21 ounces.
> *U.S. SMALL*—at least 18 ounces.

Bear in mind, if you are buying eggs for use in a particular recipe, such as a cake, a meringue, or for some other whipping purpose, that you will need more SMALL eggs than LARGE ones to achieve the same quantity of whipped whites.

Egg quality is also sometimes Federally graded. This grading (Federal or other) is done by candling—examining the egg through a powerful backlight strong enough to reveal the character of its contents. The Federal grades—and the way you can judge the rank of an egg that does not happen to carry a grade mark—are:

U.S. GRADE AA—top quality; yolk well-centered; clear and firm white, with little air space; when the egg is broken onto a plate, the rounded yolk sits high on thick white. Likely to have excellent flavor.

U.S. GRADE A—still good quality, but not quite attaining the perfection of GRADE AA; some of the white of the egg may, for example, be somewhat thin. Flavor will be good.

U.S. GRADE B—a decent-quality egg, equal to GRADE A for many cooking purposes, though not for, say, boiling or frying. Broken on a plate, the yolk will be markedly flatter, the white thinner.

U.S. GRADE C—an acceptable egg for cooking, but likely to be inferior in flavor, so suitable for uses where the flavor is unimportant.

GRADES AA and A are, essentially, the grades of choice for dishes where the egg per se is featured: boiled eggs, poached eggs, fried eggs. GRADES B and C are less suitable for those purposes, but fine for use in baked dishes, custards, sauces (GRADE B is often an excellent buy, in fact, for such uses); GRADE B may be quite acceptable even in scrambled eggs, where other flavorings are often included. GRADE C should generally be relegated to other uses.

The prices of eggs are based on a combination of these

factors. While size doesn't equal quality, both size and quality will affect the final price per dozen—which is why GRADE B eggs may be a very wise buy for use in a baked dish where the amount of egg, rather than its entrancing flavor, is important.

Eggs retain their quality, whatever that may be, so long as they are fresh. Freshness is a difficult characteristic to determine, to say the least. As a general guideline: fresh eggs tend to look dull; a shiny egg is either not fresh, or it has been washed, a procedure that removes the natural protective coating that keeps it fresh, so that if it is fresh now, it may not remain so for long. Choose dull eggs, if you can.

Sometimes, egg cartons will be dated. If they are dated, they may carry a perfectly understandable calendar date. Or, they may carry a mysterious number which does not appear to be a date at all—but it is. If the tape or paper sealing a carton bears such a number, it is very likely a day of the year. There are 365 of those, 366 in a leap year, and one way to indicate the date is to number all the days of the year, 1 through 365 (or 366). January first is thus 1 (sometimes appearing as 001), February 15th is 46 (or 046), November first—if the year is not a Leap Year—becomes 305, and so on; many calendars and appointment books note such things, and when you're egg-shopping, it's a good idea to check your calendar.

However it is indicated, the date—if there is a date—marks the day of candling, not the day of arrival in the store (all egg dealers do inspect their own merchandise for basic quality before releasing it for retail sale). Try to buy, if eggs are customarily dated in your area, within a week of the candling date.

Eggs may occasionally contain specks or blood spots; if you like, you can remove these (except for cooked-in-the-shell eggs, of course) before using the eggs. These are biological abnormalities that do not normally affect either flavor or nutritive value.

IV. Guide to Shrewd Shopping:
Fresh Fruits and Vegetables

Generally speaking, fresh fruits and vegetables are more economical than canned or frozen ones—if you buy when the item's abundant (and therefore low in price), and if you develop enough judgment to choose good quality, whatever you pay; high quality means economy here, because it's a matter of greater use, less waste per item or pound.

The U.S. Department of Agriculture does have quality grades for fresh fruits and vegetables; they're rarely used, however, except as a basis for wholesale trading, and with few exceptions, the consumer is not likely to encounter graded produce. From the consumer viewpoint, quality depends on a number of factors: the original condition at harvest time; care in handling and (in some cases) packaging; time elapsed between harvest and point of sale; and the conditions maintained throughout. Natural deterioration in many instances can be rapid—but can be effectively countered by knowledge and skill during the stages between grower and buyer.

Prices are usually lowest when a local or nearby crop is abundant—but this isn't necessarily true, if the item is regularly shipped from some other area. (If you are interested in gearing produce purchasing to growing and shipping schedules, the USDA will help: its Market News Service provides such information to local news media, and its Consumer and Marketing Service issues monthly bulletins detailing plentiful foods, therefore probably good buys; write the USDA, in Washington or locally, to obtain these materials.) Obviously, high price does not necessarily equal high quality, nor low price low quality.

The USDA has issued a nine-point buying guide for fresh fruits and vegetables; the author cannot improve on it. Somewhat condensed, it follows:

(1) Inspect the merchandise personally.

(2) Don't let low price alone persuade you to buy, unless the low price is the result of overabundance.

(3) Consider local and nearby production times and seasons.

(4) Don't buy more than you can keep and use without spoilage.

(5) Don't buy low-quality merchandise just because it's low-priced; it may be far from a bargain, because of waste.

(6) Remember that size doesn't necessarily equal quality.

(7) Learn to distinguish between defects of appearance alone and those that actually affect eating quality; many blemishes are removed in normal preparation.

(8) Make sure that you receive full measure for your money—and that you peek beneath the top layer of produce sold in containers.

(9) Use care in your own examination of produce; "rough handling in the process of selection," the USDA properly points out, "causes spoilage and waste for which consumers as a group must pay."

The descriptions that follow—fruits first, then vegetables, items arranged alphabetically within each category—indicate what types you may choose from, what factors constitute quality merchandise, and in many instances what characteristics may be telltale clues to undesirability.

Bear in mind that all this must be weighed against your personal preferences and inclinations; you may not find less-than-ideal flavor or texture, for example, objectionable—but the price should in such circumstances be less than top drawer as well.

FRUITS

Alligator Pears: see AVOCADOS.

Apples: Apples, unlike most fruits and vegetables, are often graded, which is quite a help in selection. The three grades indicate meeting of minimum standards; ungraded apples may meet these standards (grading is optional), but there's no guarantee.

Apples from the Far West are usually packed to meet state grades, in descending order: EXTRA FANCY, FANCY, and GRADE C.

Apples grown east of the Rockies usually, if they are classified, bear U.S. grades (again in descending order): U.S. EXTRA FANCY, U.S. FANCY, U.S. NO. 1.

Some types of apples are especially suited for eating as is, others for other purposes. Among the prominent varieties:

BEST FOR EATING (also good for cooking)— Delicious, Golden Delicious, Jonathan, MacIntosh, Stayman, Winesap. In late 1968, a new variety called the Jonagold—a hybrid developed by mating the Golden Delicious and Jonathan types—was announced by the New York State Agricultural Experiment Station; it is said to be distinctive in size and flavor.

FAVORED FOR PIES (tart and slightly acid)— Gravenstein, Lodi, Newton (Albemarle Pippin), Yellow Transparent.

ESPECIALLY GOOD FOR BAKING (largest most

suitable)—Northern Spy, Rhode Island Greening, Rome Beauty.

Generally speaking, a good apple for its type has good color, is firm and free of bruises, and clean. Fairly common deficiencies are evidenced as follows:

Apples picked at an immature stage will lack color, and may look shriveled after a period of storage; their flavor tends to be poor.

Overripeness is evidenced externally by ready yielding to slight pressure; the flesh of such apples will be soft and mealy, their flavor inferior.

"Scald" is caused by gases given off by the apples themselves during storage or transit; it occurs—though infrequently—during winter and spring, and affects green varieties more than highly colored types. Scald is evidenced by irregular brownish areas on the surface of the apple; if mild, it has only a slight effect on overall quality, but if severe (darker and more widespread), its effect can be serious.

Early damage in the form of freezing or bruising is evidenced by external softening (the flesh beneath will be mealy and brown), as is breakdown due to other causes. There is likely to be extensive waste in buying such apples.

Decay or insect damage is likely to be obvious; because apples are now so widely graded, such damage is far less prevalent than it used to be.

Apricots: Good-quality, properly matured apricots are plump and fairly firm, colored a uniform golden orange; such apricots are usually juicy and flavorful.

Greenish-yellow apricots, unusually hard and perhaps slightly shriveled, are immature, and will be noticeably lacking in flavor. Bruised ones are immediately edible (except for the bruised parts) but tend to deteriorate extra-quickly. The beginnings of decay are evidenced by softness (in advanced stages, mushiness), a dull appearance, and possibly shrinking or shriveling; when decay has started, the flavor has already deteriorated to a considerable extent.

Avocados: Now available all year round, avocados (also called alligator pears) come in many varieties of size, shape, and texture, none of which have any relationship to quality or flavor (and pay no attention to any advice along those lines; those suggesting that you should buy avocados only when they are green, or brown, or some other color, are simply familiar with only one variety or those produced in one area). Their shapes can range from near-spherical to pear, gourd, egg, or bottle; their sizes, from 5 ounces to 2 or 3 pounds (8 ounces to 1½ pounds are the most common); their colors, from light green through darker or mottled green to near-black dark brown; their skin texture from dull to shiny, from super-smooth to coarse and pebbly.

Avocados are ready to eat when they are ripe—which is never prior to picking, for they (unlike most fruits) will not ripen on the tree. If you want to eat it right away, look for one that yields to gentle pressure near the stem end; if you don't, get an entirely firm one (it will ripen in two to five days at room temperature). If the avocado is extremely soft to start with, it is past the ideal edible stage and its flesh will be mushy and probably discolored; properly, the flesh is buttery, somewhat soft, with a delicate nutlike flavor.

Bruises or cuts through the skin are likely to affect quality; dark, sunken spots, with or without deep cracks, indicate decay. Avocados evidencing such defects are below standard. A light brown irregular marking called "scab," however, is a superficial defect, and won't affect internal quality.

Bananas: Bananas are deliberately harvested green,

or unripened; unpleasantly strong flavor develops if they're permitted to ripen on the plant. A fully ripe, ready-to-eat banana is deep yellow, flecked with brown. One that's green, or solid yellow with green at the tip, is not yet ripe (full flavor has not yet developed, and the banana will be hard); if the skin is entirely brown, it's gone beyond the edible point (though occasionally—especially if the banana itself is still fairly firm—such a banana will still be good to eat). If you plan to use bananas right away, get ripe ones; if not, get some that haven't fully ripened, and let them ripen at room temperature.

Aside from degree of ripeness, plumpness and freedom from bruises are evidence of quality; strange discolorations and obvious bruises indicate low quality, probably extensive waste, and fast deterioration. Bananas with none of the previously described characteristics, but evidencing a rather old, dull look, were probably overchilled at some point and won't ever ripen properly or develop full flavor. Mold, especially in combination with discoloration, is evidence of decay.

Berries (including Blackberries, Boysenberries, Dewberries, Loganberries, Raspberries, and Youngberries): Good-quality berries of these multiple-cell types are plump and of uniform good color, free of moisture, dirt, leaves, or stems; they have a bright, clean look. If a few cells of some berries are green or off-color, it's not a serious defect, but the flavor is likely to be inferior; adhering caps indicate underripeness and immaturity, and again, the flavor is apt to be undeveloped.

Other characteristics can evidence more serious defects, in the direction of overripeness and decay. Mold is a definite indication. Other clues are soft, crushed, or wet berries, which aren't always evident when produce is packaged in a wooden or cardboard container; watch for wetness or stains, check sides and bottom, and spill out berries to check lower layers. Even if only some berries have been affected, the presence of any unusable ones means waste.

Blackberries: See above.

Blueberries: Top-quality blueberries are plump and fresh-looking, clean and dry, of a full, deep color and fairly uniform size throughout the container. "Bloom," a slight to quite noticeable light-colored natural protective film sometimes overlying the true dark hue, doesn't detract from quality.

A lifeless look, softness, plus possible shriveling mean the berries are old and overripe. As with other berries, beware of the stickiness or stained container that indicates breakdown and decay, or the mold growth that means the fruit is definitely over the hill. Again, spill out berries to check lower layers.

Boysenberries: See BERRIES.

Cantaloupes: Maturity is the essential characteristic to look for in cantaloupes, evidence that the fruit was harvested at the proper time; such cantaloupes develop sweetness, full flavor, and fine texture. The rind of a mature cantaloupe is ash-gray to yellow-gray or buff, with a coarse "netting" pattern that stands out from the surface; there are no bits of stem still adhering to the stem end. A poor netting pattern, a greenish cast to the rind, the presence of part of the stem (or a deep, irregular scar resulting from its being yanked off forcibly) are all clues to too-early harvesting, and a cantaloupe that's likely to be tough in texture, lacking flavor.

It may be hard to tell when a cantaloupe's ripe and ready to eat (though a reliable, experienced grocer can give good advice). Usually—though not always—there's a distinctive aroma. Slight softening at the blossom end is a dependable sign; the problem is that such softening can be induced by the repeated pressure of a number of inquisitive thumbs. Allover softness, normally accompanied by definitely yellow rind, means the melon is overripe; the flesh has at this point gone soft and watery, and flavor has deteriorated. A shriveled or flabby cantaloupe is decidedly not fresh, and the flavor will be objectionable.

Surface mold or mildew anywhere other than the stem end is a minor defect, unlikely to affect eating quality. Severe bruising, however, causes mushiness at the point of injury, and if it is extensive is likely to mean considerable waste. Penetrating decay is evidenced by soft, sunken spots, or by the presence of mold or moisture at the stem end.

Casaba Melons: Casabas are normally nearly round, but may be somewhat pointed at the stem end; the rind is wrinkled or furrowed lengthwise. They are harvested late, and usually ripened in storage, so that a casaba melon should generally be ready to eat when it arrives in the store. At this stage the rind is yellow, and there is a slight softening at the blossom end of the fruit; the flesh will be creamy white, thick, and juicy. Dark, sunken, wet-looking areas, whether or not accompanied by mold, are signs of decay.

Cherries: There are two kinds of fresh cherries generally available—the sweet eating types, and the sour or "tart" ones best for use in pies and other cooked dishes. All are in season from May through August.

The principal sweet types, grown mostly in the Far West, are the dark mahogany Bing and Lambert; the purplish-black Black Tartarian, Republican, and Windsor; the purplish-red Schmidt; the Royal Ann (Napoleon), light golden with a pinkish blush. Royal Anns are light-fleshed, the others dark.

Chief tart types, grown mostly in the Great Lakes area and some parts of the East, are the clear medium-red

Early Richmond and Montmorency, and the deep blood-red English Morello.

Quality cherries, of whatever category, have a bright look, plumpness, and good color for their particular type; sweet ones should be firm, sour ones fairly firm. Cherries that are small and unusually hard, with poor color, are immature; they'll be deficient in juice, overly acid in flavor. Soft, shriveled, leaky ones are stale, and don't buy cherries that are bruised or cut (as with berries, beware of damp or stained containers)—there will be rapid decay and development of mold.

Chestnuts: Those that are freshest and have the best flavor are heavy in proportion to their size, with tight-fitting shells.

Cranberries: There are many types and variations in cranberries; most commonly sold are the large, bright-red tart ones, and the smaller, darker, usually sweeter types. Both are generally available through the fall and winter months.

Good, fresh cranberries are plump and firm, with a high luster; if they've been in cold storage, they'll appear somewhat moist for a short period thereafter, with no ill effects. Dull, soft, shriveled, or off-color berries are decidedly inferior, and stickiness usually indicates injury, with resultant internal leatheriness and discoloration.

Crenshaw Melons: These melons, pointed at the stem end and rounded at the blossom end, mature late in the fall and are usually ripened in storage. The rind is generally smooth, though it may be slightly ribbed, and of a mottled green and gold hue that gradually becomes less green as ripening proceeds. The flesh of the fully mature melon is soft, sweet, and juicy, pale orange in color.

The rind of a ripe crenshaw melon is a bright, deep golden yellow (though there may be a few still-green areas), and the melon yields very slightly to moderate pressure, especially at the blossom end; there is usually a pleasant aroma as well. Check carefully for sunken, "water-soaked" areas; this is evidence of decay, which spreads rapidly into and through the flesh of the melon.

Dewberries: See BERRIES.

Figs: Because figs are extremely perishable, very little of the crop—grown mostly in California, partly in Texas and the Southeast—is shipped fresh. A fully ripe fresh fig is soft or fairly soft, varying in color from greenish yellow to purplish black, depending upon the variety. Figs quickly turn sour and start to ferment, a condition that is readily apparent because of its unpleasant odor; any bruising or breaking of the skin serves to speed this deterioration still more.

Grapes: Two basic types of grapes are commonly available.

The European or Vinifera type, grown in the West and especially in California, is the higher in sugar and solids content, and tends, with some exceptions, to be somewhat larger. Some varieties are seedless; if there are seeds, they separate readily. Principal varieties are Almeira, Cardinal, Emperor, Flame Tokay, Malaga, Muscat, Red Malaga, Ribier, and Thompson Seedless.

The American type is grown mainly in the eastern and central states; principal varieties are Catawba, Concord, Delaware, Fredonia, Moore Early, Niagara, and Worden.

Top-quality grapes of either type are mature, plump, and fresh-looking, and are firmly attached to their stems. (Shake the bunch gently before you buy; marked "shattering"—falling of many grapes—means dry, brittle stems, and the grapes are not fresh.) Generally, high color is a key to good flavor and sugar content, except that white and green grapes are often at their best when they are beginning to turn amber; a few varieties of the American type, however, remain green when fully ripe.

A few defective grapes—small, wrinkled, sunburned, or unripened—don't render the entire bunch inferior. Mold, wetness, or signs of rotting near the stems, though, are signs of decay—which does affect the bunch as a unit.

Grapes injured by freezing will be objectionably flat in flavor. Eastern or American ones so injured are usually shriveled, their pulp milky and opaque. Western or European grapes evidence such damage by a dull appearance, stickiness, and a tendency to shatter badly; additionally, when a grape is pulled off its stem, the small bunch of fibers left on the stem will be discolored and shorter than normal.

Grapefruits: There is extensive variety in types and colors of grapefruit commonly available. Rind colors range from pure yellow to overcasts of reddish brown, brown, or red-gold (Florida and Texas growers often use the term "bright" to denote the clear yellow, "russet" or "bronze" to describe variations); the flesh may be white or pink; some varieties are seedless, some not. All these are matters of personal preference, have no special bearing on quality or flavor.

Good grapefruits are well-shaped, heavy for their size, firm but springy; soft, flabby, or unusually light fruit is inferior. The heaviest and smoothest usually have the thinnest skin and the most juice. A slight point at the stem end, especially if the skin is rough or ridged, usually means thicker skin, relatively less juice.

Surface scars, scratches, or discolorations can generally be overlooked so far as quality goes. Any sign of decay, however, means that the flavor has been affected, and that the taste will be flat and bitter. Such signs are softness, with or without discoloration, at the stem end; a "soaked"-looking area anywhere on the fruit, usually accompanied by discoloration, with the peel in that area soft and easily broken off; any mold whatever.

Honey Ball Melons: These are small, round melons whose rinds bear a lightly "netted" pattern reminiscent of cantaloupe; their flesh, when ripe, is light green and sweet. As with cantaloupe, maturity is essential; a deep stem scar means the melon was harvested too early for proper maturing. Ripe honey balls have a grayish-yellow to light yellow rind, yield slightly to pressure.

Any bruises or cracks mean that the flesh beneath them has been injured in terms of both texture and flavor. Mold, or areas that are dark and sunken, are signs of decay.

Honeydew Melons: Substantially larger than the similarly named honey balls, honeydews are about the size of the crenshaw melon, weigh from 4 to 8 pounds, and are bluntly oval in outline. Their whitish-green rind—usually smooth, occasionally with traces of a "netted" pattern— turns to a creamy white or yellow with full ripeness; the flesh, like that of honey balls, is pale green and sweet. Undamaged honeydews keep quite well, and can be held for ripening; watch for the color change, plus a slight softening at the blossom end. Don't buy melons with any signs of damage or decay: severe bruises, cuts, sunken spots with or without odd-colored dotting.

Lemons: The best ones are firm and brightly colored, heavy for their size, with fairly fine-textured skin. Those of a deep yellow hue are usually juicier and less tart than paler yellow ones or those with a slightly greenish cast; look for the latter if you prefer the tarter type. Don't-buy signs are shriveling or hard skin (signs of age and dryness); softness and sponginess (signs of internal injury or deterioration); "water-soaked" spots; mold; a soft, off-color area at the blossom end (the last three signify decay).

Limes: Look for firm limes with good green color, fairly heavy for their size; those of a somewhat yellowy hue may be lacking in desirable tanginess of flavor. Purplish-brown irregular spotting, which sometimes occurs, may or may not be significant; sometimes the lime is defective internally, often it is not. Other signs of age, injury, and so on, are the same as those for lemons (above).

Loganberries: See BERRIES.

Mandarin Oranges: See TANGERINES.

Melons: See specific type.

Muskmelons: See CANTALOUPE.

Nectarines: For top quality, choose plump, clean, fresh-looking nectarines, firm but not hard, and with good color—usually orange-yellow to red, but sometimes green, depending on variety; some varieties may display a yellowish to brownish "staining," but if there are no other defects, the fruit will not be affected internally. A nectarine is at its best for eating when there is a slight softening at the most prominent side area, vertically along the "seam."

A really hard nectarine may be immature (usually it is then dull-looking and a little shriveled, too) and in that case its texture will be leathery and it will never develop decent flavor; hardness may also indicate a simple lack of ripeness, though, and such fruit will ripen in a day or two at room temperature. A soft nectarine, however, is definitely overmature and well along the road to decay; any cracks mean it is highly subject to rapid deterioration; and wetness suggests that decay has already begun.

Oranges: There are a number of varieties on the market

from various growing areas and at different times of the year, far too many to list here. Principle sources and types:

From California and Arizona: Washington Navels, available from November to May, seedless and with segments that separate easily, therefore popular for eating; Valencias, in season from May through the fall, which have few seeds but thinner skin and a great deal of juice. Oranges from the California-Arizona area are usually of a deeper orange color than the eastern varieties.

From Florida (and some from Texas): Parson Browns and Hamlins, available in late fall; Pineapples and Temples, in season from December to March; Florida Valencias, shipped from March through June. Oranges from this area are often russeted, a color deviation which has no effect on flavor; sometimes the peels are dyed—a harmless cosmetic procedure—and are then stamped "color added."

Recently, hybrids—such as the "Tangelo," a cross between orange and tangerine—have appeared on the market as well.

Quality oranges, like other citrus fruits, are firm, have good color, and are heavy for their size. Puffy or spongy ones, light in weight, are poor quality and deficient in juice; wilted, shriveled, or flabby ones are extremely old or have sustained some internal injury. Decay is evidenced by soft surface areas with a "soaked" look that may break under pressure, or by mold.

Papayas: Under- or over-ripeness are the papaya pitfalls. A properly mature fruit is golden yellow to orange in color, and yields slightly to pressure. Super-softness, or mushiness, or any dark spots are symptoms of age and decay.

Peaches: Most of the peaches sold for fresh use are of the yellow-fleshed freestone type. Clingstones, though sometimes sold fresh, are used principally for commercial canning; there are both white- and yellow-fleshed varieties within each of the two types, but the latter are the more popular. (There are also intermediate types known as "semi-freestones" and semi-clingstones.")

Because peaches are highly perishable, they are usually picked at a mature but still-hard stage for long-distance shipment. Look for bright and fresh-looking fruit, cream to yellow in color (there may or may not be a "blush" of red). A ripe peach is fairly firm; if the fruit feels overly firm, but the color is right (no green), ripening is likely to proceed properly, and you needn't hesitate to buy it (though not for instant eating). Fruit that has been snatched off the tree too soon, though, won't ever ripen or achieve proper color; it will become shriveled or flabby, the flesh will be tough and rubbery, the flavor extremely bad.

Unusually soft peaches are overripe, and should be purchased (assuming there are no other defects) for immediate use only. Bruised fruit is a bad buy; the flesh beneath the bruised spot is apt to be soft and discolored. Brown spots are signs of decay—and in the case of peaches, it moves fast, and spreads readily to adjacent pieces of fruit as well.

Pears: The main and most popular pears in the American market are the familiar Bartletts, in season from late summer through fall; after that many stores offer one or more of the other available varieties, principally Anjou, Bosc, Comice, Flemish Beauty, Garber, Keiffer, Seckel, and Winter Nelis.

The best-quality pears are picked when they are mature but still hard and green; they are then usually ripened under optimum conditions by the wholesaler (though if bought not quite ripe, they can be ripened at room temperature as well). Tree-ripened pears tend to offer inferior flesh texture, rather coarse and gritty. Those picked too soon, before the mature stage, will never ripen properly; they'll tend to shrivel, and will be deficient in both texture and flavor.

Choose pears that are clean, without cuts or bruises, well-shaped and fairly firm to firm (but not hard). They soften as they ripen; one that yields very easily to pressure at the stem end or sides is quite ripe, and should be eaten immediately. Color will vary from one variety to another and is not necessarily an indication of either quality or ripeness; some pears in prime condition are light green or greenish yellow, while others may be entirely yellow and still not ripe; "russeting," a reddish-brown blush, is normal in some varieties, not in others.

Do examine the fruit for definite skin discoloration; if it is extensive, decay has probably begun (mold is also a sure sign of decay). Check, too, for "water-soaked" areas (the flesh is likely soft and mushy beneath them) and for dark brown rough spots (pronounced ones may signify woody spots in the flesh). Anjous, the most widely sold winter variety, are also subject to "internal cork spot," a corky-flesh condition evidenced externally by small lumps and green spots.

Persian Melons: Somewhat like cantaloupes in appearance and texture, but larger, Persian melons also display a "netted" pattern on their rind, though somewhat finer and flatter than that of cantaloupes. Their flesh, like that of cantaloupes, is sweet, fine-textured and orange-colored when the melon is fully ripe—a condition indicated externally by slight softening at the blossom end, a faint aroma, and a change in the color of the rind from green to gray-green or bronze-green. Soft, sunken spots, or patches of mold or moisture at the stem end, mean decay.

Pineapples: There are three principal varieties of pineapple offered in U.S. markets, differing considerably in the color of the ripe fruit: Red Spanish, which may be reddish brown, light orange, or golden yellow; Smooth Cayenne, ranging from light yellow to deep golden yellow; and Sugar Loaf, a Mexican variety that remains green when ripe. All are picked in a mature-but-hard stage. A pineapple picked too early is dull light green to greenish yellow in color, has a somewhat dry or shriveled appearance with "eyes" underdeveloped; it will never ripen properly, and its flavor will be highly acid and unpleasant. If the fruit is mature, it will be firm and bright and—if it is top quality— heavy in relation to its size; the ripe fruit has developed the right color for its type and has a distinctly pineappley odor, especially when one of the leaves is plucked from the top.

Don't buy a pineapple that's sunburned, with a distinctly lighter-colored area on one side; the flesh beneath the burn will be hard, dry, and pithy. Discolorations are bruises, and a bruised pineapple is apt to soften and decay fast. And watch, too, for these warning signs of underway decay (which, once begun, is an especially speedy process in pineapples): mold; an unpleasant odor; moisture; a soft, watery area, either at the base or around any of the "eyes."

Plums: Major varieties are Beauty, Becky Smith, Burbank, Duarte, Eldorado, Kelsey, President, Purple Plum, Reine Claude (Green Gage), Santa Rosa, Shiro, Standard Prune, Tragedy, and Wickson. (Prunes are, of course, dehydrated plums; varieties used are those with pits that separate readily from the flesh when the fruit is ripe, so the plum may be dried without removing the pit.) Some varieties are yellowish green when ripe, others orange-red or purplish black.

Good-quality ripe plums are plump, clean, and fresh-looking, soft enough to yield to slight pressure, and have developed good color for their type. A hard or shriveled plum is immature, will never ripen or develop good flavor; one that is very soft and leaky is overmature and on the verge of decay (if the plums aren't sold loose, watch for moist or stained containers). Sunburn appears in plums as brownish blotches; such fruit is likely to have inferior flavor. Cracked plums (unless the cracks are fully healed) are a bad buy; the cracks are open invitations to decay organisms.

Raspberries: See BERRIES.

Strawberries: Don't select strawberries by size; this factor has nothing to do with flavor or quality. Many varieties of strawberries have been developed to suit differing soil and climate conditions, and each differs a bit from others in size or flavor; none is inferior to the others, though.

Good strawberries are fresh, clean, dry, and bright-looking, with a full red color. Unlike many other berries, strawberries should have the cap and a bit of the stem attached; capless berries are highly susceptible to mold and decay. Extremely small and misshapen berries often have hard green areas and poor flavor.

Moldy strawberries are decayed (and be sure to tip the container to check out berries beneath the top layer), and such decay is obvious. Be alert to other signs of overripeness, age, imminent spoilage—berries that appear dull or shrunken, or are soft and moist (as with other berries, stain at sides or bottom of the container signals old, leaky berries inside).

Tangerines: Mandarin oranges are one type of this popular eating fruit with its easy-to-peel skin and easy-to-separate segments. Because the skin is normally loose, tangerines are not necessarily firm to the touch (pronounced softening at the stem end, however, is a sign of rotting). Choose those that are bright and clean, deep yellow to deep orange in hue, heavy in relation to their size. Mold, of course, is a definite mark of decay; a distinct lack of luster is a suspicious sign, too.

Watermelons: It's important to get a melon that's ripe and mature—something even an expert finds it next to impossible to discern from the outside. Most markets sell half- and quarter-melons—and sometimes smaller sections as well—so you can examine the inside. Quality criteria are firm and succulent texture, a good red color, and seeds that are dark brown to black. Light-color flesh and white seeds mean the melon is immature and lacks flavor and sweetness, while flesh that is dry and mealy, or watery and stringy-looking with some darkening around the seeds, tells you that the melon is either overmature or very old, in either case not good eating. A problem of decay is unlikely in a freshly cut melon, but do check the outer surface of the rind for penetrating injuries. The one other occasional watermelon defect is "white heart"—a white streak in the flesh running lengthwise through the melon; melons so afflicted will have extremely bad flavor.

Youngberries: See BERRIES.

VEGETABLES

Artichokes: What's under discussion here is the globe artichoke, also known as the French artichoke, the unopened flower bud of a plant of the thistle family (the Jerusalem artichoke, a potato-like tuber occasionally used for pickling, is seldom seen in the retail market). In the U.S., it is produced chiefly on the West Coast.

A prime-quality artichoke is compact and plump, heavy in relation to its size (though size per se is not equivalent to quality or flavor), and its leaf scales are large, fleshy, tightly clinging, and—most important—green (with either age or injury, they will become brown—and tough). If the leaf scales are hard-tipped, or if the center of the artichoke is fuzzy and purplish, it is overmature; its leaves will be tough, and the flavor will be too strong. Bruises (dark, off-color areas), mold growth, or other discoloration often means that the artichoke will turn black when it is cooked. Check the base of the artichoke for worm injury; though it might appear negligible, don't buy an artichoke with wormholes—because small worm injury outside may signal serious damage inside.

Asparagus: The white part of the asparagus stalk is the below-the-ground part; the asparagus is cut when the above-the-ground part has reached the desired length. (Those white sections are usually tough, but they are quite usable in soups.) Top-quality asparagus is both tender and firm; the tips are closed and compact; cut ends are moist (and the store should properly see that they are kept that way). Fresh asparagus should be used quickly, as it ages fast, the tips spreading or wilting and the stalks acquiring an objectionable woody quality. Asparagus that is angular or flat in shape is usually tough and woody to begin with.

Beans, Green: See BEANS, SNAP.

Beans, Lima: Usually classed as large or small, lima beans may be sold either in their pods or shelled. Pods should be clean, bright, fresh-looking, dark green in color, and above all, well-filled; flat pods contain too-young, immature beans; a dried-up, shriveled, spotted, flabby, or yellowing pod is either old or diseased, and contains tough beans with inferior flavor. Any sunken areas, whether or not mold is present, are signs of decay.

Shelled limas should be plump, green to greenish white in color, with tender skin (test it by puncturing; hard, tough skin means old beans, with objectionably bad flavor). Examine them closely; shelled beans are quite perishable, and can become moldy fairly quickly.

Beans, Snap: There are many varieties. Some are green, others yellow (wax beans); some are flat, some oval in cross section, others round. Which you choose is a matter of personal preference. Their family name, though, is a criterion of freshness for all, for fresh beans are firm and will snap easily and crisply when broken; good-quality fresh beans should also be reasonably well-shaped and free of scars. When you break a bean to check crispness, take a good look at the inside. If it's lifeless and wilted, the beans have been hanging about too long since harvesting, and flavor's likely to suffer; if it's soft and watery, and/or moldy, the bean's decayed; if the seeds are on the large side, the cooked beans will probably be somewhat tough and fibrous. Most snap beans, whether they're termed "string" beans or "stringless," are in fact relatively stringless; all of them get stringy, though, when they're overmature.

Individual bean length isn't related to quality. An assortment of beans that are about the same size, though, will cook more evenly.

Beans, String: See BEANS, SNAP.

Beans, Wax: See BEANS, SNAP.

Beets: Beets may be sold in small bunches tied together by their tops (usually the early crop), or individually with their tops removed (usually the later crop); late-crop beets of medium size are often a little better in flavor than very large or very small ones. The condition of the tops or leaves of beets sold in bunches has nothing to do with the quality of the beets themselves, though if the tops happen to be in good shape (not discolored or yellowing), they do make good greens (also see the next listing). As to the beets, simply make sure that they are smooth and firm; any sign of softness or wetness means they're decaying.

Beet Tops: Though the tops of young beets may be used (see BEETS), tops separately sold are usually ones that have been specifically grown and harvested for this purpose; you'll occasionally find a small, undeveloped beet attached. Beet tops should be clean, fresh, and tender—though if they're just slightly wilted, they can usually be revitalized in cold water; don't buy them if they're slimy or soft and watery. (Also see GREENS.)

Belgian Endive: See CHICORY.

Broccoli: The name used alone denotes the tender young stalks, branches, and bud clusters (for broccoli leaves, see GREENS); the heads may vary from 1 to 5 inches in diameter. There are several varieties, and color may range from dark green to sage-green or purplish green. Look, in any case, for broccoli with a fresh, clean appearance, stalks and branches that are tender but firm, and definitely compact bud clusters (open clusters with yellow blossoms are overmature). Wilted, flabby, or yellowed broccoli is not fresh; brittle, woody stalks are a sign of old age, and will be spongy and flavorless when they are cooked.

Brussels Sprouts: These look like miniature cabbages, and the brussels sprout is in fact a cousin of the cabbage, botanically speaking. Fresh sprouts are usually on the market from fall through spring. They should be firm-to-hard, compact, and of a good, bright green hue. Soft, puffy ones have gone—or are going—bad; wilted or yellowed sprouts are old, and there is likely to be a lot of waste in preparing them. Keep a sharp eye out for worm-eaten leaves. Also be on the alert for sprouts with a smudgy or dirty look; such markings are the trails of aphids, plant lice that have invaded inner surfaces—at best causing undue waste, at worst making the entire sprout unfit to eat.

Cabbage: Various types of cabbage are generally sold; the five principal ones:

POINTED—has a conical head; is often marketed as "early" or "new."

DANISH—usually white; matures relatively late; has a hard, tight-leaved, compact head which, when viewed from the stem end, appears circular.

DOMESTIC—round or on the flat side, somewhat less compact than the Danish; there are early, mid-season, and medium-late varieties.

SAVOY—includes a number of varieties with round, or "drumhead," shaped heads, and finely crumpled leaves.

RED—includes several different varieties; distinguished by color.

Prime-quality cabbage of whatever type is solid and firm (though "early" cabbage is normally not quite so firm as the later crop), heavy in relation to its size, and closely trimmed—the stem cut close to the head, with very few outer leaves remaining. If some outer layers have separated from the stem, and are held in place only by compact folding over the head, the cabbage is still of good quality, but may tend to have a somewhat strong flavor or coarse texture.

Common cabbage defects are worm damage (examine the head carefully for holes), yellowed leaves, burst heads, and decay. Don't buy cabbages seriously affected by such defects; if the defect is slight, the head can sometimes be trimmed with little waste. Yellowed or otherwise discolored leaves, however, usually signal extensive damage inside the head.

Carrots: Most of the crop is packed with trimmed tops in small bunches, or in plastic bags with the tops removed entirely. Select firm, fresh carrots that are well-shaped and well-colored; soft or shriveled ones are of distinctly inferior quality, and carrots that are forked or seriously cracked can entail considerable waste. Soft or wet-looking spots, with or without mold, are signs of decay.

Cauliflower: When the cauliflower is shipped, the leaves are usually trimmed to just beyond the curd (the edible flower portion), with the leaf-stems left to protect the curd; sometimes, though, more of the stems are trimmed away, and a paper or plastic wrapping is used for protection—so the number of leaf-stems may vary, and has no connection with the quality of the cauliflower. Nor is size a criterion; there is considerable variation.

The curd should be white to creamy white in color, firm and compact, and any outer leaf portions present should look fresh and green; small leaves within the curd don't affect quality, nor does a ricey or granular look to the curd itself (so long as the flower clusters are not spreading). Don't buy bruised or discolored cauliflower, and watch for telltale smudges and specks that mean an infestation of aphids (plant lice).

Celery: Celery sold in the U.S. is chiefly the green Pascal type, though a few markets also offer the Golden (blanched) type. Choose celery that is fresh, crisp, and clean, with good heart formation; the branches should be brittle enough to snap easily, the leaves fresh-looking. Soft, pliable branches will have a pithy quality; undersized, unusually hard branches tend to be stringy or woody. "Seed-stem," a solid round stem instead of the usual heart formation, means that the celery's flavor may be unpleasantly bitter.

Be sure to separate the stalks and check for the presence of insects or insect damage, and for a special celery affliction called "blackheart," evidenced by black or brown discoloration of one or more of the small heart branches or leaves.

Chard: Chard, also called Swiss chard, is a special type of beet grown for the tops only. The stalks should be fleshy but not coarse, the leaves fresh and crisp and free of insect damage or other injury; yellow leaves or other discoloration means the chard is old. Wilting leaves will be tough and stringy.

Chestnuts: See FRUITS

Chicory, Endive, & Escarole: These salad greens, though differing in appearance, can all be judged by similar standards. Endive and escarole are both flat, spreading plants; escarole leaves are broad, however, while endive has narrow, curly, finely divided leaves. Chicory is broad-leaved, and while still a spreading plant, is more upright than endive or escarole; the leaves of blanched chicory (also known as Witloof chicory, Belgian endive, or French endive) are folded, and form a nearly solid, elongated head.

Look for crisp, fresh, tender leaves, twisting a leaf to determine this; tough, coarse leaves will have an objectionably intense, bitter flavor. Unblanched leaves should be green (blanched chicory should be creamy white). Wilted chicory, endive, or escarole can sometimes be freshened in cold water, but there is often excessive waste involved. Brownish color or sliminess indicates decay.

Collards: See GREENS.

Corn: Corn is usually precooled after harvesting and shipped under refrigeration; it will lose flavor and tenderness fast if kept at warm temperatures, or if there is undue delay between harvesting and consumption. Watch for fresh shipments (or the appearance of a new local crop) in your market.

Choose well-filled ears, with fresh green husks; the husks should be on, though they are sometimes cut back to permit examination of the corn itself. The kernels (which may be white or yellow, depending on variety; most commercial production is of the latter type) should be bright, plump, and slightly resistant to pressure; when you break one with your fingernail, it should release a milky fluid. Of course there should be no worms or other infestation.

Corn with dry, yellowed (or straw-colored) husks or dry, shrunken kernels is old and stale; extremely large, hard kernels mean the corn is overmature and tough. Very soft, small, underdeveloped kernels mean immature corn, harvested too early, which will be lacking in flavor.

Cress: See GREENS.

Cucumbers: Select cucumbers that are well-shaped, firm, bright-looking, with a good green color (some varieties normally have a small amount of whitish green at the tip and on the ridged seams). A withered or shriveled cucumber will be tough and somewhat bitter; one that looks dull and puffy, and has turned yellow, is fine for pickling, but is no longer fit for fresh use. Decay appears first as spots with a "water-soaked" look, in more advanced stages as irregular sunken areas, possibly including mold.

Dandelion Greens: See GREENS.

Eggplant: A good-quality eggplant is firm, heavy in relation to its size, free from scars or cuts, and of a uniform dark, rich purple hue (except of course if it is of the white variety, rarely available). Wilting, shriveling, or flabbiness usually means bitterness or some other flavor defect. Check carefully for wormholes; if you find any, there is probably extensive internal damage. Decay appears as dark brown spots, and once it has appeared, it progresses rapidly.

Endive, Escarole, French Endive: See CHICORY.

Garlic: Garlic is occasionally sold with tops, but usually the tops have been removed; the bulbs are sometimes offered individually, sometimes packaged in pairs in small boxes that are partly transparent. Each bulb consists of many cloves (the number may vary); the bulb has an outer skin, and each little clove has its own papery skin as well.

The bulb should be clean, dry, and compact, with—if the garlic is prime quality—its outer skin unbroken. If the outer skin is split, however, the garlic may still be fine; just make sure the individual cloves inside are still plump and uninjured, with their own individual skins intact (breaks there may mean sprouting has started, and that will be waste). Don't buy a garlic bulb that's soft or spongy, whatever condition its outer skin may be in; there is either sprouting, or some kind of internal injury, or decay in process. Mold is also evidence of decay. A bulb that's shrunken or shriveled has fallen victim to dry rot, a kind of decay that starts at the top of the bulb and moves downward until all the contents are powdery and useless.

Greens: This general term includes a number of leafy things—collards, leafy broccoli, cress, dandelion and mustard greens, turnip tops, et al—used as a vegetable like spinach, or in salads. Look for greens that are young, crisp, and fresh-looking, with a good green color. Avoid produce that's insect-nibbled, coarse-stemmed, dry, yellow, flabby, or wilting.

Herbs, Green: In purchasing parsley and other green, leafy herbs, follow the same criteria as for GREENS (above); be sure what you buy is fresh, with good color for its type, and not stale or wilted.

Kale: See GREENS.

Leeks: See ONIONS, GREEN.

Lettuce: There are four types generally available in U.S. markets:

CRISP-HEAD or ICEBERG lettuce, the most common type, has a large, solid head with fringed outer leaves that are large and medium green in color, and paler inner leaves folded into a compact mass.

BUTTER-HEAD lettuce has a smaller, rosette-like head with relatively smooth, soft, light-colored leaves. Common varieties are Bibb, Big Boston, and White Boston.

COS or ROMAINE lettuce has a tall, cylindrical shape with long, folded, very dark green leaves.

LOOSE-LEAF lettuce doesn't form a head at all, consequently doesn't ship well over long distances and is usually sold only locally. Its leaves range from light yellow-green to dark green or a reddish green, depending on the variety.

The last three types are not hard to judge, since it's easy to examine individual leaves; be sure they're clean and fresh, with no discoloration, insects or insect damage, or signs of decay.

In iceberg lettuce, pick a head that's fairly firm to firm, the leaves that you can see clean and crisp; avoid heads with rusty or brown-tipped outer leaves (usually signifying a similar condition inside) or areas that appear "water-soaked" or discolored (signs of decay, which usually penetrates deeply into the head). Inspect the head, too, for evidence of advanced seedstem growth—wide spaces between the bases of the outer leaves and/or a strange swelling at one side near the top of the head—which will mean a good deal of wastage in removing it, as well as bitter flavor in the remaining lettuce.

Lima Beans: See BEANS, LIMA.

Mushrooms: Top-quality mushrooms are clean and fresh-looking, white to creamy in color, with no pitting, wilting or discolorations; sizes can range from about ¾ inch to about 3 inches in diameter. The caps shouldn't be open, strictly speaking, and won't be if the mushrooms are absolutely fresh; if they are partially open, though, just to be sure that the gills (the fluted area between the cap and stem) are still light in color, and haven't turned brown or black.

Mustard Greens: See GREENS.

Okra: Okra, the immature seed pod of a plant of the Hibiscus family, is used chiefly for soups. The pods should be about 2 to 4 inches long, tender, clean, and fresh-looking, and should snap easily; they may be green or whitish green, depending on variety. Dull and dry-looking pods are old; they are usually woody and fibrous, with hard seeds. Pods that are shriveled or discolored are not fresh, and will lack flavor.

Onions: There are four general classes of onions widely available (in addition to the necked types, separately considered in the next listing):

BERMUDA—a large flattish type, sweet and mild in flavor, usually in markets from March through June; there are yellow, white, and red varieties.

SPANISH or VALENCIA—large but elongated, also offering mild flavor, commonly available from August through April; includes light yellow, white, and brown varieties.

GLOBE—includes a number of types, all roughly globular in shape, generally fairly strong in flavor, but variable; there are yellow, white, red, and brown varieties. Globe onions are available throughout the year.

BOILERS—really part of the previous class, these are the small white globe-shaped onions usually cooked whole rather than chopped or sliced like most of the larger types.

Whatever the type, choose onions that are bright, clean, hard, well-shaped for their type, and dry-skinned. Wet, discolored, or moldy areas are decayed; moisture at the neck is evidence of internal decay.

Misshapen onions—such as "bottlenecks" or "doubles"—are not inferior in taste or texture, but are likely to involve waste in preparation, and are thus unwise buys. Seedstem growth means there will be substantial waste; it is evidenced by a visible green stem or by a thickened, tough, or open neck.

Onions, Green; Leeks; Shallots: Green onions (also called scallions, or spring onions) are early white or bulbless varieties deliberately harvested at an immature stage. Leeks, similar in appearance but much larger (the base is usually about an inch in diameter), have straight white necks and broad, dark green solid leaves; their flavor is relatively mild. Shallots, another related species, have straight stems and very slight bulb development when they are harvested before maturity for use as a vegetable (the small bulbs of mature shallots are usually chopped or minced for use as a flavoring element; see Chapter VI).

In selecting any of these, look for a crisp, tender quality, necks that are very light in color for at least 2 or 3 inches, and tops that are fresh and green. If the tops are yellowing, wilted, or discolored, the necks are likely to be tough and fibrous.

Parsley: See HERBS, GREEN.

Parsnips: Top-quality parsnips are on the market only in the winter and early spring; because their flavor does not develop fully until after prolonged exposure to temperatures of 40° F. and lower, they are usually stored under refrigeration after they are harvested, kept in storage until they are ready for sale. Choose parsnips that are smooth, clean, firm and well-shaped, small to medium in size (very large ones are apt to be tough and woody at the core). Avoid those with soft or shriveled roots, usually indicating a fibrous texture. Soft spots on the parsnip, usually but not always accompanied by mold, are symptoms of rotting.

Peas: It's vital to be sure that the peas you purchase are fresh; they lose their sweetness and flavor fast. Young, tender peas are found in fresh-looking pods of light to medium green; the pod should feel slightly velvety to the touch, and should be well-filled (though not bloated or swollen). Taste one of the raw peas; it should be tender and sweet.

A flat dark green pod with a wilted look will contain tiny, immature peas with undeveloped flavor. A swollen pod, one that's yellowy or whitish, or perhaps flecked with gray, houses old, tough, flavorless peas. The presence of "soaked" spots of mildew on the pod augurs considerable waste.

Peppers: There are two major types available. Sweet peppers are generally of the "bell" type, though the shapes can actually vary considerably, and are usually sold at an immature deep-green stage; they change to bronze or bright red as the maturing process continues. Hot (Chili and Cayenne) peppers are sold in either the green or the red stage, usually the latter, and range in size from quite small to nearly as big as the bell type; they are sometimes displayed dried and strung together.

Fresh peppers should be firm and bright-looking, with

thick flesh; the calyx (leaf cup) should be fresh and green, whatever the color of the pepper itself. A very soft, pliable, pale-green pepper is immature. One that is fully developed in color but shriveled and dull-looking, or one whose calyx is wilted or darkened, is not fresh. If there are any spots that are bleached or blackened, or that have a "water-soaked" appearance, the pepper is decayed; peppers with any injuries penetrating the wall should be shunned too, since they are highly susceptible to rapid decay, and internal decay may have already begun.

Potatoes: There are four general types of potatoes on the market, most of which are sold both "new" and later in the year. "New" potatoes are dug before they have fully matured, and are shipped immediately; since they are more delicate and subject to injury, their skins often have a ragged look (which, if there is no other injury or defect, does not detract from their quality). The later crop is stored and shipped through subsequent months. The four types:

ROUND WHITE—principal varieties are Cobbler, Katahdin, Kennebec, and Sebago; Katahdins are chiefly late crop, the others marketed both "new" and later.

LONG WHITE—the main variety is the White Rose, produced mostly but not entirely in California (potatoes of this variety from that state are usually referred to as "California Long White"); most are offered for "new" sale, though some are stored and sold later.

RUSSET—the most prominent variety is the Russet Burbank, whose shape is generally elongated; it is considered especially good for baking, is marketed from storage from late summer to late spring. Other principal varieties are the Russet Rural, a generally round potato, also sold from storage, and the Early Gem, a variety bearing a strong resemblance to the Burbank, which is sold as both "new" and late crop.

RED—includes many varieties; the principal ones, all round, are Red Pontiac and Red La Soda (both sold "new" and from storage), Red McClure (chiefly late crop), and Bliss Triumph (chiefly "new").

If your menus often include potatoes in various kinds of dishes and forms, experiment a bit to find the types you like best for various uses.

In purchasing potatoes of any type, choose those that are firm, fairly smooth, and of reasonably good shape, and avoid those with unusually deep "eyes," necessitating a good deal of waste in peeling and preparing; reject any that are wilted, seriously discolored, spongy, or beginning to sprout. Wet or rotting spots are decayed, though if the area's quite small, it can be cut away with little waste; it's impossible to tell, on the other hand, how extensive the damage may be inside—so if possible, avoid buying potatoes with any decay spots.

A distinct tinge of green on one side of a potato is evidence of either sunburn or "lightburn" caused by too-long exposure to either natural or artificial light; if the burn is extensive, the potato may have a bitter taste.

Potatoes are subect to internal afflictions, principally "hollow heart" (a hollow center) and "blackheart" (internal black areas); such conditions can't be diagnosed from external examination, but if shippers and dealers are reliable, the problem should seldom if ever arise.

Radishes: There are many varieties of radishes, but most of the ones commonly available are the round red varieties about ¾ inch to 1¼ inches in diameter; some are sold in bunches with their tops, others trimmed and packaged in plastic bags. Good-quality radishes are firm, smooth, well-formed, and crisp; they will be tender, with mild flavor. Don't buy spongy or wilted ones, or those that show signs of decay. But don't be deterred by small cracks or bruises, or skinned areas; these are simply the result of mechanical harvesting, and they are no special drawback if the radishes look good otherwise.

Rhubarb: Rhubarb sold early in the new year is hot-house-grown, chiefly on the West Coast and in Michigan, and is usually light pink to pale red, with yellow-green leaves. The field crop, available in late spring and early summer, is normally a dark, rich red. Whatever the color, fresh rhubarb should be firm, crisp, tender, bright-looking, and neither too thin nor too large; younger stems will have the most delicate flavor. Wilted or flabby rhubarb isn't fresh, will have poor flavor and stringy texture. Over-size stalks with poor color were harvested too late; they will be very tough, and much will be wasted.

Romaine: See LETTUCE.

Rutabagas: See TURNIPS.

Scallions, Shallots: See ONIONS, GREEN.

Spinach: Spinach is sold whole, also in the form of cut-up leaves packaged in plastic bags. If you are buying it whole, look for plants that are well-developed and stocky, neither straggly nor overgrown. The leaves, in either case, should be clean, fresh, and tender, with a good green color—not wilted, bruised, or yellow (though in the whole plant, there may often be some small yellow-green undeveloped heart leaves). Decay in spinach appears as soft, slimy disintegration.

Spring Onions: See ONIONS, GREEN.

Squash: There are many varieties of squash, with wide variation in color, size, and shape; they fall into two main categories, each including a number of types.

Summer, or soft-rind, squash may be classed by color types:

WHITE or CREAMY WHITE—the most common variety is the White Bush Scallop (also called Cymling or Pattypan), smooth and disk-shaped, with scalloped edges.

YELLOW varieties are usually elongated-bulbous shapes with a warty rind, designated as Straight- or Crook-Neck.

GREEN, green-black, and green-striped varieties are generally elongated, cylindrical in shape, include Zucchini and Italian Marrow.

Summer squash is at its best in an immature stage, with tender rind and small seeds; if it is let go to the hard-rind stage it develops hard seeds and stringy flesh. Choose those that are fresh-looking, fairly heavy in relation to size, and free of cuts or bruises.

Winter, or hard-rind, squash is generally divided seasonally:

FALL and EARLY WINTER varieties commonly available are Acorn, Danish, and Des Moines (green, corrugated), Butternut (buff), Delicious (green or golden).

LATER WINTER varieties, of which there are a large number, tend to be larger in size; colors include several shades of green and orange, and there is considerable variety in texture. The deep-gold-to-green Hubbard is perhaps the most popular type.

In winter squash, the hard rind is important; softness is an indication of immaturity, a watery quality, and lack of flavor. Winter squash is especially susceptible to decay; reject those with any "water-soaked" areas, whether or not any brown or black mold growth has yet begun.

String Beans: See BEANS, SNAP.

Sweet Potatoes: There are two types of sweet potatoes, offering somewhat different flavor and texture; which you choose is a matter of personal preference—but for uniform cooking results, be sure that you don't have a mixture. The types:

PORTO RICO and NANCY HALL VARIETIES, commonly called yams, have the higher sugar content; when cooked, their flesh is moist, deep yellow to orange-red in color. Their skin color may range from whitish tan to rosy or brownish red, and they are plumper in shape (though that can vary).

JERSEY-TYPE sweet potatoes, when cooked, tend to be firmer, drier, somewhat mealy; their flesh is light yellow to pale orange. Skin color of this type is yellowish tan or fawn, and the potatoes tend to be less plump in shape (but again, it varies).

Quality sweet potatoes of either type are clean, smooth, firm, and well-shaped. Extensive cracks or an unusually misshapen potato usually mean a good deal of waste. Decay is a special problem with sweet potatoes; it spreads fast within the potato, can spread to other specimens as well—and will impart a disagreeable flavor to unaffected parts of a potato, even if the decayed area is cut off. Examine sweet potatoes carefully for signs of decay, with particular attention to the ends, which tend to be most quickly affected. Symptoms to watch for: soft wet rot; dry rot; discolored, shriveled, or shrunken areas; greenish-black spots; mold growth.

Swiss Chard: See CHARD.

Tomatoes: Tomatoes may be ripened either before or after picking, and are grown in many areas, so are available year round. Those that are shipped are generally picked green but mature enough to ripen under the proper conditions; most long-distance shipments are ripened under controlled temperature and humidity conditions, then packaged. Others are harvested at what is known as the "breaking" stage, when the color is starting to change to pink, and these tend to be more flavorful. But the best flavor is offered by vine-ripened tomatoes; thus tomatoes grown locally are most desirable.

Fresh, ripe tomatoes should be well-formed, plump, free of bruises, and of a uniform red color. Any scars, roughness, or well-healed cuts on the skin will not affect internal quality, though these surface blemishes will have to be removed in preparation. If there are unhealed cracks (with no other defects), buy the tomatoes only for immediate use; ripe tomatoes are in any case susceptible to decay, and any opening to the interior multiplies the possibilities.

Tomatoes that are puffy, lightweight, and oddly angular will have inferior flavor and may involve extensive waste in preparation. Reject any that display wormholes or decayed areas (evidenced by softness, discoloration, or mold).

Turnips: There are various turnip crops. The early crop, marketed during the winter months, tends to be small and tender and is sold in bunches with tops or with tops partly cut back. The late—or main—crop is usually larger and marketed with tops removed, sometimes after storage. Rutabagas are a species of the turnip family; they are large and elongated, with yellow flesh and a distinctly different flavor, but the selection guidelines are essentially the same.

Look for smooth, firm turnips, heavy in relation to their size, with few leaf scars around the crown, and very few roots at the base. They should be free of wormholes. If there are tops, they should be fresh and green. A soft or shriveled turnip is likely to be tough eating; one that is large and overgrown, especially if it is light for its size, will probably be tough and pithy and/or overly strong in flavor.

Turnip Tops, Watercress: See GREENS.

Witloof Chicory: See CHICORY.

Yams: See SWEET POTATOES.

V.   Keep It Fresh, Keep It Fair

Storing your food so it stays in optimum condition is our subject here—and with certain foods, it can sometimes be a puzzlement. A detailed alphabetical listing follows; first, some general guidelines.

For packaged food that's still unopened, you're generally safe in going by the store's display method. Things in jars and cans can be kept, by and large, on a cabinet shelf (unless of course you'd rather refrigerate them, as a matter of personal preference; the author, as it happens, always refrigerates canned fruits). Anything from the store's meat or dairy cases should go into your refrigerator. Any frozen food should be stored in your freezer.

Once a can or jar has been opened, however, it's wise to refrigerate it (whether or not the label or lid so specifies) and, in the case of canned food, to transfer its remaining contents to a jar with a lid. The food will keep for quite a while under airtight original-packaging conditions, but exposure to the air makes the situation quite different; air may act on the metal of a can, too, hence the transfer to a jar.

Fresh foods are of course the main problem. The list below covers most of them (as well as some packaged, cooked, and leftover items). Bear in mind that fresh food, ideally, is intended for immediate use; though a food may keep—unless otherwise noted—several days under refrigeration (which, incidentally, means a temperature under 40°), its quality does deteriorate a little each day, and the storing measures you take—except for freezing—will simply retard that gradual deterioration. Do be sure to check Chapters III and IV to be certain the food in question is fresh to start with; criteria for ripeness will also be found there.

A final note concerning freezing. Your freezer should be kept at zero degrees; keep tabs on the temperature (and that of your refrigerator as well) with one of the special thermometers made for this purpose. Meats—or any other foods you freeze at home—should be tightly wrapped, with air bubbles squeezed out, in heavy foil, plastic, or freezer wrap; flexible freezer wrap is far better than the paper kind (plastic bags can be used, too). If frozen food has been thawed but is still quite cold, it can be refrozen, though there will be some loss of quality; if it has been warmed to room temperature, use it immediately or discard it.

If you do not find a fresh food covered in this list (look for both the specific food and its overall category), and there is some question in your mind about its keeping qualities, the rule is: when in doubt, refrigerate.

Apples: Wash in cool water, dry, and refrigerate.

Apricots: Refrigerate, but don't wash until you're ready to eat.

Asparagus: Swish through cold water, trim any scales under which sand may still be lodged, and refrigerate in a plastic bag or covered container. Deterioration, even under refrigeration, is fairly rapid; try to use within a day.

Avocados: If they're not yet ripe, keep avocados at room temperature until they're ripe; if they're ripe, refrigerate them to retard further softening, unless you intend to eat them the same day. If you want to eat only half an avocado, what to do with the other half so it will keep and not turn black is to leave the pit in; sprinkle lemon juice over the exposed flesh; cover it with plastic wrap, and refrigerate it.

Bacon: See MEAT, CURED.

Bananas: If not yet ripe, let them ripen at room temperature. If they're ripe and you don't want to eat them immediately—or if they're not, and you want to slow down the ripening process—put them in the coolest room in your house. Don't refrigerate bananas; the extreme cold darkens them.

Beans, Snap: Refrigerate in a covered container or plastic bag, but don't wash them until you're ready to cook.

Beef: Refrigerate, following the rules for MEAT, for use within three days. If later use is intended, freeze (will keep for one year).

Beets: Remove the tops and refrigerate in a covered container or plastic bag.

Berries: Sort, then refrigerate the ones you want to keep; don't wash until you are ready to use. Check often for signs of mold.

Bread: May normally be kept, still in its store-bought wrapper, in a tightly closed bread box at room temperature; if you and your family eat very little, however, keep it in the refrigerator to retard the formation of mold. Bread may also be frozen, and will keep in the freezer up to three months; freeze it in small packages of a few slices, rather than freezing the whole loaf in one large package.

Butter: Refrigerate it, covered; that latter point is vital, since butter readily absorbs other food odors. If you buy butter (or margarine) in pounds made up of quarter-pound sticks, keep the currently-in-use stick refrigerated in a covered dish, the other sticks in the freezer, to be brought out as needed.

Cabbage: Refrigerate it, wrapped or bagged in plastic.

Cake: Should be eaten the same day, since it will tend to dry out. Uneaten portions should be plastic-wrapped or covered, and refrigerated. Some cakes may be frozen: un-iced cupcakes and muffins (they'll keep, frozen, for three months), fruitcake (will keep for a year).

Carrots: Remove any tops, wash and dry (but don't scrape until ready to use), and refrigerate them, either wrapped or in the vegetable bin or crisper.

Cauliflower: Refrigerate, wrapped or covered.

Celery: Wash, trim off any bruised or defective portions, shake off excess water, and refrigerate in vegetable bin or crisper.

Cheese: Refrigerate in its original wrapping, if it's packaged cheese (if it's not, and it comes wrapped in paper, rewrap it tightly in plastic); once opened, rewrap the remainder tightly in plastic (not foil, which can adversely affect some cheeses). Dried-out cheese pieces may be grated for use in omelets, as toppings, etc.

Cheese, Grated: Keep in a securely closed jar in the refrigerator.

Cherries: Refrigerate; wash and dry first, if you wish.

Chicken: See POULTRY.

Coffee, Ground: Keeps its flavor and aroma best if it's refrigerated in a tightly closed container. If it comes in a paper sack, transfer it to a jar or canister.

Coffee Beans: Refrigerate in an airtight container.

Cold Cuts: Refrigerate in the original wrapping, if the packaged variety (if not, rewrap in foil or plastic); once open, rewrap the remainder in foil or plastic. Cold cuts will keep, refrigerated, five to seven days.

Cooked Food: Refrigerate, wrapped or covered; the amount of time it will keep varies, depending on the food, but a few days is average. (Note: When refrigerating cooked poultry, package the meat, gravy, and stuffing separately.) Many cooked dishes may also be frozen, and will keep that way four to six months. A casserole dish or stew may easily be cooked for this specific purpose, simply by doubling the amount you make and cooking in two different containers: line the one you plan to freeze with heavy foil before cooking, let the food cool after cooking, then put the whole business in the freezer; when it has frozen solid, lift the frozen food out of the container, take the container out and store the foil-wrapped package in the freezer (it will fit neatly into that same container for reheating). Something cooked specifically for freezing (unless it is a dish, like some stews, that can benefit from extra cooking) should be undercooked by 25 percent.

Cookies: Keep at room temperature in a cooky jar or other closed container. Cookies may be frozen for later use, keep about six months that way; if they're home-baked, cool them to room temperature before freezing.

Cooky Dough: May be frozen unbaked, and will keep about four months. To freeze, roll it out, cut the cooky shapes, stack them with wax paper between, wrap the stack in freezer wrap.

Corn: Refrigerate, but don't remove the husks until you're ready to cook it.

Cornstarch: Handle the same way as FLOUR.

Cucumbers: Wash, dry, and refrigerate, but don't peel until ready to use. When you have used part of a cucumber, refrigerate the remainder (still unpeeled) and cover the cut end with wax paper or plastic.

Dough, Pastry: May be made up as much as a week ahead of time and kept in the refrigerator in an airtight wrapping (plastic wrap works best).

Eggs: Refrigerate; store as they come in the carton, with the broad end up, to keep the yolk centered. Never wash eggs; washing removes the natural protective coating that helps keep their fresh quality.

Egg Whites: Leftover whites for which you anticipate future use will keep for about two weeks in the freezer; freeze them in foil molded into a pan shape, sealing the top after the whites have frozen solid.

Egg Yolks: Yolks will keep in the refrigerator for two or three days; put them in a small bowl or jar with enough cold water to cover (slide them in and out very carefully).

Fats: Refrigerate in a covered container.

Fish: Refrigerate as soon as you get it home, in a dish or plate, loosely covered with wax paper, on the bottom shelf of the refrigerator—and use it the same day. If you don't plan to use it that very day, freeze it for later use (it will keep six months); the easiest way, if the fish is not too large, is to make a tray by cutting a milk carton (quart or 2-quart) in half vertically, place the fish in it, fill with water, and freeze.

Flour: Will keep in a cupboard, but switch it from its paper sack to a tightly covered canister or large jar to keep it dry and to protect it from infestation by worms or insects.

Frankfurters: Refrigerate, well-wrapped (keep in the original package until you use—then rewrap any remainder in plastic); will keep for about a week.

Fruits, Citrus: Refrigerate if your room temperature is normally above 65°.

Fruits, Dried: Keep in a tightly closed container, and refrigerate if room temperature is normally above 65°.

Fruits, Fresh: If not yet ripe, let them ripen at room temperature—then, generally (except for bananas), refrigerate. (Note: also see listings for a number of individual fruits.) Don't attempt home freezing of fruits; it's true that some can be and are frozen commercially—but this is super-fast (below zero) freezing, and must be done within hours of harvesting.

Fruits, Frozen: Frozen fruit packages have a freezer life of about one year.

Garlic: Keeps at room temperature, need not be refrigerated. Garlic may also be frozen, if you wish, by separating the individual cloves (but not peeling them) and keeping them in a covered jar in the freezer.

Grapes: Refrigerate in a covered bowl or plastic bag, but don't wash them until you're ready to serve them.

Grapefruit: See FRUITS, CITRUS.

Greens: Handle the same way as CELERY.

Ham: Refrigerate for use within one week; frozen, will keep for one month.

Hamburger: Refrigerate in a dish or bowl, loosely covered with wax paper, on the lowest shelf of the refrigerator; use within two days. Frozen, hamburger will keep two to three months, and you can make it into patties first, if you like: either wrap each patty separately, or place slices of wax paper between them so they won't stick together.

Herbs, Dried: Transfer to an airtight container, if they didn't come in one, and keep away from heat and strong light. For more information, see Chapter VI.

Herbs, Green: Are best used immediately, if possible (also see separate listing for PARSLEY)—or dried by spreading out on a towel or hanging up (not in direct sunlight) for about a week, then stored as above.

Honey: Keep tightly covered (and wipe sweet drippings off before capping and storing in the cupboard); it's best not to refrigerate honey, since extreme cold often causes crystallization (if that does happen, though, the honey can be melted again by setting the jar in hot water).

Ice Cream: Put into the freezer immediately; it will keep for a month. Once the package is opened, put a piece of wax paper on the surface to prevent ice crystals from forming.

Jams & Jellies: Refrigerate after opening.

Juices: Refrigerate; once a can has been opened, transfer any unused portion to a covered jar.

Juice Concentrates, Frozen: Will keep for a year in the freezer; you can put a can of juice concentrate into the refrigerator rather than the freezer if you are going to use it within a day.

Ketchup: Refrigerate after opening.

Lamb: Refrigerate (see MEATS) and use within two days, or freeze; frozen lamb keeps for three to six months.

Lard: Refrigerate in a covered container.

Lemons: See FRUITS, CITRUS.

Lettuce: Wash in cool water, trim off any defects, drain (let sit for a while in a colander or washing basket), then refrigerate in crisper or vegetable bin.

Limes: See FRUITS, CITRUS.

Margarine: Handle the same way as BUTTER.

Mayonnaise: Refrigerate after opening.

Meat, Cured: Refrigerate in its original wrapper if packaged; if not, rewrap securely in foil or plastic. Will keep seven to ten days in the refrigerator, one month frozen.

Meat, Fresh: Refrigerate on a dish or plate, loosely covered with wax paper (tight wrapping will promote faster deterioration), on the bottom (coldest) shelf of the refrigerator. Don't leave meat in the butcher-store paper; the paper absorbs some of the meat juices, and also slows up the chilling of the meat.

Meat, Smoked: Handle the same way as MEAT, CURED.

Melons: If not ripe, let ripen at room temperature; when ripe, refrigerate if your room temperature is normally above 65°—preferably in a plastic bag, since melons can easily absorb other food odors. After a melon has been cut, be sure to cover the cut surface with a sheet of plastic wrap.

Milk, Condensed or Evaporated: Unopened, need not be refrigerated; after opening, transfer any unused portion to a covered jar, and refrigerate. Condensed milk so kept will last a very long time, weeks or even months, but evaporated milk's refrigerator life is approximately that of fresh milk.

Milk, Fresh: Keep refrigerated, unless you specifically want it to sour.

Milk, Nonfat Dry: Keep in a securely closed container, but need not refrigerate; when it is liquefied, however, it should be treated as fresh milk.

Milk, Whole Dry: Refrigerate in a closed container.

Mushrooms: Refrigerate in a plastic bag.

Nectarines: Refrigerate; may be washed and dried first, if you like.

Nuts: In shells, need not be refrigerated; once shelled, should be refrigerated in a covered container.

Olives: Refrigerate after opening; if in a can, transfer to a covered jar.

Onions, Dry: Keep at room temperature.

Onions, Green: Refrigerate, wrapped or covered.

Oranges: See FRUITS, CITRUS.

Parsley: Wash, shake off excess water, and refrigerate in a large covered jar or in the crisper or vegetable bin.

Parsnips: Refrigerate.

Peaches: Refrigerate, but do not wash until you're ready to eat.

Peanut Butter: Keep tightly covered, but need not refrigerate; it can be kept in the fridge if you like, but tends to get hard and difficult to spread.

Pears: Refrigerate; wash and dry first, if you wish.

Peas: Refrigerate; it's best not to shell them until you're ready to cook, but if you have to do the shelling ahead of time, put the shelled peas in a covered container.

Peppers: Wash and dry, and refrigerate.

Pickles: Refrigerate after opening.

Pineapples: If not ripe, let ripen at room temperature; when ripe, refrigerate if your room temperature is normally above 65°.

Plums: Refrigerate; wash and dry first, if you wish.

Pork: Refrigerate (see MEATS, FRESH) for use within two days; frozen pork will keep for three to six months.

Pot Liquor: Keep in a covered jar in the refrigerator.

Potatoes: Need not refrigerate, but keep out of direct light—either sunlight or artificial light—to prevent "lightburn."

Potatoes, Mashed: Refrigerate leftover mashed potatoes in a straight-sided glass; when thoroughly cold, they can be cut into potato cakes and fried.

Poultry: Refrigerate in the same way as MEATS for use within two days; if an extremely large bird will not fit in the refrigerator, it will very likely be all right for that day or two if it is kept where the temperature is consistently below 50° (outdoors in cold weather, for example). Frozen poultry will keep for four to six months. Individual pieces may be conveniently frozen by packing them into an ice tray—then, when they have frozen, transferring the frozen block to freezer wrap.

Radishes: Wash, remove any leaves, and refrigerate. After serving, any leftover radishes that have been cut into "rosettes" should be discarded.

Salad Dressing: Refrigerate.

Sandwiches: To keep overnight, wrap individually in wax paper or plastic sandwich bags, and refrigerate. Sandwiches may also be frozen, and will usually keep about two or three months; be sure to wrap tightly.

Shellfish: Refrigerate, unless alive (in which case cook immediately); freeze if not using the same day (will then keep about six months).

Soup: May be made and then frozen for use within two months. Freeze in an ice tray, then transfer the frozen block to freezer wrap or plastic bag.

Spices: Transfer to airtight containers (if they don't come that way) and keep away from temperature extremes.

Spinach: Handle the same way as LETTUCE.

Squash: Refrigerate if your normal room temperature is above 65°.

Stock, Meat or Fish: Keep in refrigerator, boiling it about twice a week to keep it from spoiling. If you want to freeze it (it will then keep for several months), boil it down to about one-third first; it will take up less space that way.

Strawberries: Sort and refrigerate; don't wash or hull until ready to use.

Sugar: Transfer from the box to a covered canister.

Sugar, Brown: After opening, transfer to an airtight canister to keep it from drying out; an extra moisture-keeper is to put dried apricots into the same container—keeps the sugar soft, also gives the fruit a good flavor.

Sweetbreads: Handle as other VARIETY MEATS, with this exception: sweetbreads (calf pancreas) are extremely perishable in the uncooked state, and if they're not being used the minute you bring them home should be parboiled before refrigerating. Simmer them for fifteen to twenty minutes in water containing 1 teaspoon of salt and 1 tablespoon of vinegar to each quart of water; drain; cover with cold water; when they are cool, snip and remove the outer membrane, then place in a covered container and refrigerate (they must still be used within one day).

Sweet Potatoes: Refrigerate if your normal room temperature is above 65°.

Tomatoes: If not yet ripe, let ripen at room temperature; when ripe, wash, dry, and refrigerate.

Turnips: Refrigerate.

Variety Meats: These are internal organs such as liver, hearts, tongue, kidneys, and the like; refrigerate, and use preferably the same day, the next day at the very latest.

Vegetables: See individual listings. Vegetables may theoretically be home-frozen, but it's not recommended; the pre-freezing procedures require trickily timed blanching or steaming and a good deal of expertise. Packaged frozen vegetables have a freezer life of about one year.

VI. Index of Herbs and Spices and Other Flavor-Makers

Here are the little something extras that can add so much to the sheer fun of cooking. The fresher, the better, for most of these perker-uppers. But whether you choose to grind your own spices and grow your own herbs in garden plot or window box, or buy the packaged kind, you'll find they can bring a sense of adventure to food preparation.

Beginning cooks are best advised to follow recipe directions to the letter when incorporating flavorings. Later, when you're fully familiar with the dish in question, you can make some changes—adding and subtracting quantities, dropping flavors and adding others—to make the dish your very own creation; refer, then, to Part 2 of the index in this chapter.

Bear in mind, as you build your herb and spice shelf, that freshness is indeed a factor, and that the form and age of an herb will affect the amount you use. Generally speaking, dried herbs concentrate the flavor—so use less of the dried than you would the fresh, perhaps one-quarter to one-half the amount. Flavor degenerates, on the other hand, as time goes by; if weeks or months have passed since you purchased an herb, use more than the usual amount—and discard and replace herbs after about nine months.

The index that follows is divided into two parts. In the

first, you'll find an alphabetical rundown of herbs, spices, and other flavor-makers, and some helpful and interesting information about each, including its character and major uses and, for some, home-growing and other data. (Note: Home-grown herbs should be used as picked.)

Following that list is an index in reverse—some foods and categories of foods, with herbs, spices, and seasonings especially suited for them by flavor or tradition.

PART 1: FLAVORS

Allspice: a berrylike fruit native to the West Indies, available dried in whole or ground form; its flavor and aroma very much resemble a blend of cinnamon, cloves, and nutmeg. Whole, it's useful in pickling and also in poaching fish; ground, it's used chiefly in dessert dishes— pies, cakes, cookies, puddings.

Angelica: an herb botanically related to the carrot; its roots and fruit contain an oil used in flavoring liqueurs, and its leaf-stalks are sometimes candied as a delicacy.

Anise: like angelica, an herb belonging to the carrot family. Its seeds are the stage in which the cook is interested; their taste and aroma is distinctly licoricelike, and, like angelica, this herb is used in liqueurs. But aniseed blends well, too, with roast pork and with boiled carrots, and makes a tasty topping when sprinkled on sweet pastries and cookies.

Basil: a leafy herb botanically related to mint, but close in flavor to bay leaf or oregano; it's used fresh or dried, chiefly dried and crushed. Unless otherwise specified, "basil" appearing in a recipe mean sweet basil, the type normally used in cooking. It's good in soups, stuffings, and salads, adds something to stews and chops, is practically indispensable in any dish (such as spaghetti sauce) involving tomatoes, with which it has a special affinity; of course basil is often an important factor in Italian dishes. And it's sometimes included as one of the *fines herbes,* as well as in *bouquet garni.*

Basil is one of the herbs that can be easily attempted by the window-box gardener. It needs a good dose of sunlight, but thrives with moderate levels of humidity and watering, and can grow in a pot (even one shared with a larger plant) as well as in a garden.

Bay Leaves: the small, aromatic leaves of a European species of laurel (there are American bay leaves as well, but the flavor is different, and the imported ones are preferable). They're available dried, in either whole or crushed form; the former is more widely used (¼ teaspoon of the crushed form is equal to a whole medium-size leaf). A bay leaf—or two or three—is a good addition to soups and stews, as well as to certain meat and fish dishes baked or braised with a sauce; the leaves are always removed and discarded after cooking is completed. Bay leaf is a standard component of a *bouquet garni.*

Bouquet Garni: a combination of leafy herbs used as a flavoring unit in soups, stews, sauces, and other long-cooking dishes and removed when cooking is completed— a traditional element in French cuisine. If fresh herbs are used, they are simply tied together; if dried, crushed herbs are included, use a piece of clean cheesecloth, tied securely, to make a little bag for the bouquet. The standard *bouquet garni* is composed of two or three sprigs of parsley, a bay leaf, and a sprig of thyme, with other herbs added depending on the dish and the cook's own tastes: basil, marjoram, or rosemary are widely used, chervil or savory less often; sometimes a stalk of celery is included.

Burnet: a leafy herb little used now, for it must be employed in fresh form. Grow it at home if you like (it's a self-seeding flowering perennial), and you'll find its leaves, gently bruised and added to salads, herb omelets, or cream-cheese dishes, lend a delicate cucumberlike flavor and fragrance.

Caraway: an herb of the carrot family; its pungent, aromatic seeds are familiar to most of us in baked goods, chiefly rye bread. Caraway seeds can add an intriguing touch to other baked dishes, too—in biscuits and cakes, in pie crust—and to cheese dishes and spreads, sauerkraut, scrambled eggs and omelets.

Cardamom: the fruit of an East Indian herb of the ginger family, used dried in whole (seeds) or ground form. The former is used almost exclusively for pickling, in combination with other herbs and spices; the ground form is good in Danish pastries and some other baked goods, and is sometimes included in curries.

Cassia: strictly speaking, a specific tree whose bark is used as a spice and is similar to cinnamon, though somewhat more pungent; its uses are the same as those for cinnamon. The word is also—and more commonly—used for certain varieties of cinnamon itself. For practical culinary purposes, the spices are interchangeable.

Cayenne: also known as red pepper; the ground pods and seeds of the tropical capsicum plant, slightly different varieties of which provide us with chili powder and paprika. It's incredibly hot and peppery, and must be used with extreme caution and a light hand, as well as making sure beforehand that its presence won't disconcert prospective diners. Most common uses: seafood cocktails, egg dishes, some sauces and fish dishes, barbecued meat and poultry.

Celery Seed: available in seed form or ground and mixed with salt (celery salt), it lends a little of the flavor of celery with a slightly bitter but not unpleasant overtone, is good in salads (especially potato salad), soups, stews, fish dishes, meat loaf.

Chervil: another of the many herbs of the carrot family, and one of the *fines herbes;* its leaves have a delicate, parsleylike flavor and aroma, are used fresh or in dried-and-crushed form. Chervil adds a nice touch to scrambled eggs and omelets, herb butters, baked or broiled fish and chicken, sour cream and cheese sauces, creamed vegetables, salads, potato soup. Fresh chervil, like parsley, also makes a good garnish, especially for light-colored dishes.

Chili Powder: the fruit of the variety of the capsicum plant grown chiefly in Mexico and the southwestern U.S. (and known as the chili pepper), ground in combination with cumin and oregano. It's strong and peppery, though not so much so as its near-relative cayenne, and finds its widest use in Mexican-style cookery; it can be used, too, to spice up cocktail sauces, egg dishes. The famed Mexican dish *chili con carne* is not based on the powder, although some recipes use it, but is a stew combining finely chopped chili peppers with ground meat.

Chives: the leaves of the chive plant, a first cousin of garlic and onion (and sometimes called "chive garlic") that does not develop an underground bulb of any size; the leaves, fresh or dried and chopped, have a tangy but comparatively mild flavor, are included in the *fines herbes*. Use chives in salads and salad dressings, in sauces and dips, in scrambled eggs and omelets, as a zesty topping for cottage cheese, for sour cream on a baked potato.

Chives grow quickly, develop lavender flowers that make a pretty addition to vegetable garden or window box; because of their shallow root development, chives can also be added to a pot already containing a larger plant, and both will thrive. They need rich soil and plenty of sun, otherwise require no special coddling.

Cinnamon: the spicy-sweet, aromatic, nearly paper-thin bark of an East Indian tree, available in stick or powdered form. Cinnamon goes naturally with sweets and desserts— cakes, cookies, baked apples, stewed fruits, and puddings; combine it with cloves for baking ham, with brown sugar to top sweet potatoes or squash. And it's good, too, at the breakfast table: sprinkled, with sugar and butter, on toast; incorporated in pancake or waffle batter or in the eggs when you make French toast; added, by the dash, to maple syrup. Cinnamon is one of the ingredients in curry powder.

Cloves: the dried flower buds of a tropical tree of the myrtle family, a spice with a distinctive sweet and pungent flavor; they are available whole or ground. The whole buds are nail-shaped, convenient for sticking into things such as ham or spiced ham for baking, or into a large onion in the middle of a stew. Whole cloves are good for anything where a sweet-and-spicy quality is wanted, such as syrups, marinades, rich gravies (as, sauerbraten), cooked fruits. They should be removed from cooked dishes before serving, if possible, to save the diner the trouble of picking them out. A dash of ground cloves is good on sweet potatoes or squash and on braised carrots, and (usually combined with cinnamon) in puddings and other desserts.

Coriander: the dried seeds of an herb grown in southern Europe and parts of Asia, available whole or ground. The former are used chiefly for pickling; the ground add a sharp accent to sausages, some breads and buns, roast pork, and shrimp dishes.

Cumin: a small plant of the eastern Mediterranean area; its dried seeds resemble caraway in appearance and flavor, are available whole or ground. Cumin is used chiefly in combination with other flavorings, in making chili powder and curry powder; alone, it's sometimes used in rice dishes, breads, and cheeses.

Curry Powder: a mixture of ground spices developed in India and used to give a special exotic flavor to a number of different dishes, especially those characteristic of India, Pakistan, and Iran, and usually including rice as well as meat, poultry, or seafood; it is sometimes included in the main dish itself, sometimes in an accompanying sauce. Use it lightly at first; its flavor is strong and, for the uninitiated, often unbearably hot. The ingredients of curry powder vary somewhat from one maker to another, but cinnamon, cumin, ginger, mustard, and turmeric are always included; additional components may be caraway, cardamom, cayenne, cloves, coriander, mace, or pepper.

Dill: a European herb, like many other herbs a member of the carrot family; both its seeds and its leaves are useful in the kitchen, fresh or dried, whole or ground. The flavor is a bit like that of caraway. Dill is of course most famed for its function in pickling, but it's useful in other ways as well: in salads, especially potato salad; with cooked, buttered potatoes; in herb butters for pasta; in some fish dishes.

Home-growers might try this one, indoors or out; the flowering plant's fairly large, but can be held to a foot and a half or so by careful cropping; soil, water, and such needs are those of average house plants.

Fennel: another European herb that's part of the carrot family, with leaves and seeds (the latter are more widely used) having a strong, sweetish aroma and aniselike flavor. The fresh leaves work well in salads, especially seafood salads; the seeds or crushed leaves give interesting flavor to sausage, fish dishes, roast duck and goose, some baked goods. Fennel is one of the minor standbys of Italian cuisine.

Fines Herbes: a term used in classic French cooking and denoting a group of herbs that are chopped separately, then combined with chopped onion and shallots for incorporation in a cooked dish such as soup, stew, or a stuffing. Chervil and chives are always included, plus, usually, parsley and tarragon; some cooks add basil, marjoram, or thyme as well, depending upon the particular dish involved.

Garlic: a bulb herb, botanically a member of the lily family, and a very close relative of chives, onions, and shallots. The garlic bulb grows in small partitioned sections called cloves, only one or two of these (or their equivalent) generally used in a single dish, as garlic's distinctive flavor and aroma is strong and persistent (a quality much admired by some, despised by others). Garlic may be used whole (by rubbing the food with it, or incorporating the whole clove in a dish and removing it before serving), or slivered for insertion in incisions in a roast, or finely minced; or, its juices and flavor may be extracted by squeezing a clove or two in a handy clamping device called a garlic press. It is also available commercially in processed forms: powdered, minced and dehydrated ("instant minced"), ground and mixed with salt (garlic salt). Generally, ⅛ teaspoon of garlic powder or instant minced garlic is equal to a single, fairly small fresh clove. Garlic, in whatever form is convenient, is widely used with meats and poultry, in soups, marinades, stews, and salad dressings; it is a traditional part of Italian and Spanish, and to some extent French, cuisine.

Ginger: the root of a plant grown in the East and West

Indies as well as parts of Asia, Africa, and Polynesia; technically classified as an herb, but generally categorized, in Western cookery, as a spice because of its uses and its characteristic spicy-sweet, faintly exotic taste and fragrance. It is widely available in ground form, less widely—except in gourmet or Oriental food shops—whole. It is used especially in baked goods, such as gingerbread cake and gingersnap cookies, also with cooked fruits; in combination with soy sauce and other flavorings, it is incorporated in sauces and marinades to give an Oriental flavor to braised dishes such as poultry or pot roast.

Herb Bouquet: same as *BOUQUET GARNI*.

Herb Vinegars: vinegars incorporating the extra flavor of a specific herb; used in salad dressings, sauces, and marinades. Some are available commercially, but you can make your own by filling a quart jar with fresh basil, fennel, dill, tarragon, or chili peppers, pouring a basic cider vinegar over to cover, then letting it stand for a minimum of two weeks. For garlic vinegar, start with a quart of standard cider vinegar; add eight cloves of garlic, halved, eight whole cloves, and eight peppercorns. Taste the concoction after two weeks and frequently thereafter; when you find it has the strength you want, strain it through filter paper to get a clear liquid.

Jamaica Pepper: same as ALLSPICE.

Lemon Peel, Grated: available commercially and, in the author's experience, well worth having on hand for sprinkling on baked or broiled fish before cooking, to incorporate in sauces and marinades for poultry and fish dishes, to add a tasty new dimension to such baked goods as cookies, custards, and sponge cakes.

Mace: the aromatic outer covering of the nutmeg, similar in flavor; available in solid pieces or ground. It is generally used in the same sort of dishes as nutmeg, but because of a very slight flavor difference as well as being lighter in color, it tends to be used more during cooking (of fruits, vegetables, poultry sauces), less as a final touch on eggnog, custards, and such.

Marjoram: like basil, a leafy herb of the mint family—and, also like basil, occurring in several forms; unless otherwise specified, its use in a recipe signifies *sweet marjoram*, the kind normally used in cooking. Its leaves, aromatic and full-bodied in flavor, are used fresh or dried, whole or ground, in many meat dishes, especially lamb; in stews, sauces, salads, and salad dressings, definitely right in the presence of onion, with which it blends extra-well; with fish, poultry, and poultry stuffings; with many green vegetables, and also with yellow vegetables such as squash; as a *bouquet garni* ingredient. Marjoram is said, in herb lore, to symbolize joy. Grow it easily at home, in house or garden, if fairly rich soil or potting medium is available; it's an annual with pale violet flowers, tends to trailing growth, so is particularly suited for hanging pots.

Mint: the name of a large family of herbs; the one commonly referred to simply as "mint" is spearmint. Its leaves, with their familiar crisp, refreshing flavor, may be used fresh or dried and crumbled; a sauce incorporating them is also available commercially. Mint flavor is used for tea, blends notably well with lamb and with green peas, is also a happy touch for fruit salads, fruit compotes, jellies, punches and cocktails and cordials, as both flavoring and garnish. Mint is a good garden addition (and, in the author's memory, a most pleasant noncavity-causing childhood chewable), thrives best with little direct sunlight but generous watering.

Monosodium Glutamate: a flavor bringer-outer rather than a flavor adder, marketed most widely under a well-known trade name. It can, with no indications to the contrary, be used liberally on any meat, poultry, fish, or vegetable to coax out its natural flavor to the optimum. Monosodium glutamate has traditionally been heavily used in Chinese cuisine. As this book goes to press, there is apparent indication that a few individuals are hypersensitive to it, a circumstance discovered via observation of their reactions after eating Oriental food, and allegedly traceable to the monosodium glutamate rather than other factors; symptoms include severe headache plus a general feeling of discomfort. Those having this reaction, essentially an allergy, are a small minority—but if such symptoms are noted, discontinue using the seasoning.

Mustard: a sharp-flavored seed, available in whole or powdered form, used in pickling and, in the powdered form, as an ingredient in meat dishes, sauces, gravies, salad dressings, curry powder. "Mustard" appearing unqualified in a recipe means the powdered form. "Prepared mustard" denotes the familiar product sold in jars and used as a condiment with frankfurters and other meats; it is a blend of the crushed seeds, vinegar, other spices, and additional ingredients, varying from one type of mustard to another. The French type, Dijon mustard, also contains a small amount of wine.

Nutmeg: the seed of a tree grown chiefly in the East and West Indies; it has a warm, spicy-sweet flavor and aroma. Sold in whole (to be grated) or ground form, nutmeg, like cinnamon (with which it combines well), is much used in baked goods, stewed fruits, other desserts; it is often blended with other spices and herbs in sauces for meats and poultry; it is a familiar topping, both tasty and attractive, on such light, rich dishes as eggnog and custards.

Nutmeg by the dash also lends subtle new flavor to such green vegetables as string beans and spinach.

Onion: strictly speaking a vegetable, a larger relative of chives, garlic and shallots, but included here because some forms of it function as flavorings rather than foods per se. Dehydrated flaked onions ("instant minced" or "instant chopped") may be used in any recipe in place of fresh onions if they are to be combined with liquid and if the onion texture doesn't play a significant part in the dish, and are nice, by the dash, in such dishes as scrambled eggs; ¼ cup of the instant product is approximately equal to a medium-size fresh onion, chopped. For a cup of the fresh onion, use ⅓ cup of the instant; for half a cup of the fresh, use about 3 tablespoons of the instant. Onion is also commercially available in ground, dried form combined with salt (onion salt); use it to add a mild onion flavor to meat or vegetable dishes.

Orange Peel, Grated: like lemon peel, available commercially and a handy addition to recipes that benefit from a light, sweet, fruity touch: breads and muffins; puddings and other desserts; marinades and breadings for poultry, ham, pork; baked or candied vegetables such as sweet potatoes, squash, carrots.

Oregano: a leafy herb of the mint family, closely related in character and flavor to marjoram (though oregano has a somewhat zestier quality); it's widely cultivated in Mexico, is sometimes known as "Mexican sage." Oregano is a component of chili powder, finds its most familiar American uses in salads and salad dressings, Italian-style cookery, vegetable juice cocktails, fresh or cooked tomato dishes; it adds a nice touch to many meats, especially those, such as stews and meat loaf, involving flavor blends. Oregano, like marjoram, is easy to grow at home.

Paprika: ground fruit of the bonnet pepper, part of the capsicum family that also gives us cayenne and chili. Paprika's hot, bright hue belies its flavor—very mild, slightly sweet, much unlike that of its potent cousins. It's used as a colorful garnish as much as for its taste, on many light-colored foods: egg dishes, shellfish, poultry, cream soups, creamed vegetables or pale ones such as cauliflower, corn, potatoes, onions.

Parsley: a broadly useful European leafy herb, one of the **fines herbes** and a standard component of any *bouquet garni*; in herb lore, a symbol of festivity; available fresh, or in dehydrated flakes. Try parsley on baked or broiled fish; chopped, in combination with chervil or chives, in an omelet; minced in a butter sauce for noodles or spaghetti. It blends well with many meat and vegetable dishes, as well as most soups, sauces, and stuffings—and of course its clear green color makes it a lovely garnish, especially for light dishes such as chicken, rice, eggs, potatoes, anything creamed. Parsley can be home-grown in any moderate climate, attains a fairly small, manageable size with yellow flowers; it doesn't require an all-day dose of sunlight.

Pepper: the berries of an East Indian shrub, picked before maturity and dried (black peppercorns), or picked when ripe, dried, and the dark outer coating removed (white peppercorns); available whole or ground (black or white). Pepper is the most ubiquitous of the spices, is used along with salt in and on innumerable dishes, adding a hot, biting flavor touch. The white and the black pepper are nearly interchangeable in fragrance and taste, the black perhaps a little more intense. Ground pepper is both incorporated in cooking and used by the diner to season individual servings; the whole peppercorn is used in pickling, in soups and meat dishes, often in combination with other flavorings (removal after cooking is eased by enclosing them in a small cheesecloth bag). Pepper devotees will tell you that the freshly ground stuff is far superior; you may want to invest in a pepper mill, rather than a simple shaker, to accompany your salt cellar.

Poppy Seed: the seed of a European poppy, with a light, nutty flavor, used whole in and on baked goods from breads to cookies, in cheeses and cheese spreads, sometimes in salads. Poppy seeds are good, too, blended into a lemon-and-butter sauce for green vegetables such as beans, broccoli, or spinach.

Red Pepper: same as CAYENNE.

Rosemary: a shrub of the mint family, grown in southern Europe and the Middle East; its slim, small, needlelike leaves have a sweet, pleasant flavor, are available fresh or dried, whole or ground. Rosemary is a traditional symbol of remembrance or constancy, goes well with all meat and game (especially lamb and venison), blends nicely in stews and meat loaf, is a frequent ingredient of *bouquet garni*. With its small pink flowers, it makes a good addition to the home herb garden.

Saffron: the orange-yellow, pungently flavored stigmas of a species of crocus, dried and usually powdered. It yields rich color as well as exotic flavor to the food with which it's cooked, hence plays a popular role in rice dishes, especially those of Spanish or Oriental origin; it's also much used in seafood dishes, curries, fish soups and stews, and some cream sauces.

Sage: an herb of the mint family, traditional symbol of domestic virtue; its leaves have a fragrant, faintly bitter character, are available fresh or dried, whole or ground. Sage is especially fine for stuffings, blending happily with onions and other ingredients; other uses include pork dishes, soups and stews, some salad dressings. The fresh leaf is good in green salads—or finely chopped, along with parsley, in an herb or cheese omelet. Sage can be grown at home with little trouble, but is less attractive than many of the other herbs.

Salt: this common seasoning needs little comment, except, perhaps, a note of caution: use it sparingly in cooking unless you're fully familiar with the tastes of the diners involved; it can always be added at the table, but not subtracted. And when you're doubling the quantity of a recipe, don't double the salt; increase it only by half.

Savory: another European herb of the mint family; its highly aromatic leaves are available fresh or dried, whole or ground. It's useful, chiefly in combination with other herbs, in flavoring poultry and meat dishes (especially pork), in omelets, and with a few vegetables—notably beans, beets, cabbage, sauerkraut. There are two varieties of this herb, a difference significant mostly to those who are planning to grow their own. *Summer savory* is an annual, suited to outdoor growth in season; *winter savory* is a perennial, is somewhat sturdier and suited more for indoor growing. Both have attractive white-to-lavender flowers, need plenty of sun.

Sesame: the honey-colored, warmly nutty-flavored seeds of an East Indian herb, used chiefly as a tasty topping for various breads, rolls, and other baked goods; good, too, to season a potato or macaroni salad.

Shallots: members of the chives-garlic-onion family, shallots look like miniature onions and are similar in flavor, though their taste is a little more piquant, a little less lingering. They're used, usually minced, to give a mild onion flavor to sauces, stews, seafood salads, many vegetable dishes; often they're combined, at the sautéing or browning stage, with other herbs or flavorings. If they're not available for a recipe, the white ends of green onions ("scallions" or "spring onions") make a good substitute, with regular onions a last resort.

Soy Sauce: a thin sauce made by fermenting soybeans, then immersing them for a long period in brine; much used in Oriental cookery.

Tarragon: a European herb of the aster family, its leaves available fresh or dried, whole or crushed; it is one of the *fines herbes.* Delicately scented and flavored, with a slight licoricey overtone, tarragon is delicious in sauces (or simply crumbled in lemon juice) for broiling or baking chicken and fish, and in omelets and other egg dishes. Fresh, it's good in green salads. *Tarragon vinegar,* fine stuff for dressing salads, is available commercially—or, make your own (see HERB VINEGARS). Tarragon is a good, deep green addition to an herb garden, doesn't require full sunlight to thrive.

Thyme: a member of the mint family, an herb grown in temperate climes of both the Old and New Worlds, and a traditional symbol of courage. Its leaves, available fresh or dried, in whole, crushed, or powdered form, have strong, sharp flavor and aroma (use thyme a little more sparingly than some of the other herbs). Thyme is a must for a *bouquet garni,* best used in cases where a robust flavor is wanted: poultry stuffing, meat loaf, stews, some soups and seafood dishes. It grows best in somewhat sandy soil, needs plenty of sun.

Turmeric: the rootstock of an East Indian herb of the ginger family, like ginger usually classified by Western cooks as a spice; usually available dried and ground, as a yellow powder with a distinctly pleasant, very faintly sweet aroma. Tumeric is a component of curry powder;

like saffron, it lends appealing color and flavor to sauces, to rice and seafood dishes.

Vanilla: the capsule of a species of climbing orchid grown in tropical parts of the Western Hemisphere, available in two forms: the pod itself (or "vanilla bean"), and a liquid essence extracted from it. The extract, the most familiar form, is highly concentrated; it's used in cakes, puddings, and other desserts, preferably in the last stages of preparation, and a few drops go a very long way. The bean may be slit down the middle and cut in 2-inch lengths, then buried in a jar of sugar; after a few days, you will have vanilla-flavored sugar, which may then be used in place of sugar in recipes where both ingredients are specified.

PART 2: FOODS

Naturally, not all the herbs, spices, and other flavorings listed below are to be used at once, nor are all possibilities listed. The list simply indicates those traditionally, typically, or taste-wise most suited to the particular food or type of cuisine; which one or more you choose to use will depend of course on your mode of preparation, other items on the menu, and your personal preferences. Refer back to Part 1 of this index for more about the special character of each herb or spice.

Asparagus: marjoram, tarragon.

Austrian Cookery: bay leaves, caraway, chervil, chives, fennel, garlic, marjoram, parsley, shallots, tarragon, thyme. For desserts: cinnamon, vanilla.

Beans, Snap: bay leaves, chervil, dill, marjoram, nutmeg (for green beans), poppy seeds (in lemon-butter sauces), sage, savory.

Bean Soup: chives, parsley, savory.

Beef: garlic, all the leafy herbs.

Beets: bay leaves, coriander, savory, tarragon.

Biscuits: caraway.

Bisques: thyme.

Borscht: oregano, tarragon.

Breads: anise, caraway, coriander, cumin, grated orange peel, poppy seeds, sesame seeds.

Broccoli: oregano, tarragon.

Buns and Rolls: coriander, poppy seeds, sesame seeds.

Cabbage: anise, caraway, fennel, savory.

Cakes: allspice, caraway, cinnamon, ginger, grated lemon peel, vanilla.

Carrots: anise, cinnamon and cloves (combined with brown sugar in braised or glazed dishes), marjoram, grated orange peel (for candied carrots), rosemary, savory.

Cauliflower: nutmeg, paprika.

Cheeses & Cheese Dishes: burnet (with cream cheese), caraway, chervil (in sauces), chives (with cottage cheese), cumin, poppy seeds.

Chicken: cayenne (for barbecuing), chervil, grated orange peel (in breading and sauces), mace, paprika, parsley, savory, tarragon, thyme. (Also see ORIENTAL COOKERY; SPANISH COOKERY.)

Chicken Soup: rosemary, saffron, tarragon.

Chinese Dishes: see ORIENTAL COOKERY.

Chowder: saffron, sage, thyme.

Cookies: allspice, anise, cinnamon, ginger, grated lemon peel, poppy seeds, sesame seeds.

Corn: paprika.

Cream Sauces: chervil, saffron.

Cream Soups: chives, mace, nutmeg, paprika.

Creamed Vegetables: chervil, mace, paprika, parsley.

Curries: cardamom, cumin, curry powder, saffron, turmeric.

Custards: grated lemon peel, nutmeg for topping.

Dips: chives, garlic, shallots.

Duck: basil, fennel, rosemary, sage, thyme.

Dutch Cookery: bay leaves, parsley—also, many spices incorporated in Dutch cuisine in the days of the country's East Indian trade: curry powder, nutmeg (much used in fish dishes), other spices.

Egg Dishes: caraway, cayenne, chili powder, paprika, parsley (chiefly as a garnish), tarragon. In scrambled eggs: chervil, chives, minced onion. (Also see OMELETS.)

Eggplant: basil, marjoram, oregano.

Fish: allspice (for poached fish), basil, bay leaves, cayenne, celery seeds, dill, fennel, grated lemon peel, parsley, tarragon.

French Cookery: bay leaves, chervil, chives, some garlic, parsley, shallots, tarragon, thyme. The French are less addicted to heavy-handed herbing than is generally supposed.

Fruits: allspice, anise, cinnamon (especially with baked apples), cloves, ginger, mace, nutmeg, sesame. In fruit compotes: mint.

German Cookery: bay leaves, caraway, some garlic, mustard, parsley, peppercorns, sage, some thyme. For sweet gravies: cloves. For cakes: ginger, grated lemon peel, nutmeg, vanilla.

Goose: basil, fennel, sage.

Greek Cookery: bay leaves, dill, fennel, garlic, marjoram, thyme. For sweet desserts: cinnamon.

Ham: allspice, cinnamon, cloves, mustard, grated orange peel.

Hungarian Cookery: bay leaves, caraway, garlic, grated lemon peel, paprika (the most ubiquitous ingredient in Hungarian cuisine), parsley, poppy seeds.

Indian Cookery: cardamom, cinnamon, curry powder, garlic, ginger, mustard, pepper, saffron, turmeric.

Indonesian Cookery: see ORIENTAL COOKERY.

Italian Cookery: basil, bay leaves, fennel, garlic, oregano, parsley, thyme. Fennel stalks are also served, in Italian cuisine, as hors d'oeuvres, either plain or stuffed as celery might be.

Japanese Dishes: see ORIENTAL COOKERY.

Jewish Cookery: not notable for herb and spice use except in some soups and in braised dishes such as pot roast; most commonly used: dill, garlic, onion, paprika, pepper.

Kidneys: basil, caraway, rosemary.

Lamb: basil, garlic, marjoram, mint, rosemary, tarragon.

Lima Beans: marjoram, oregano.

Liver: basil, caraway.

Macaroni: basil, oregano in traditional sauces. In macaroni salad: sesame seeds.

Marinades: garlic, ginger, herb vinegars, grated lemon and orange peel, rosemary.

Meats: see specific kinds.

Meat Loaf: basil, celery seed, oregano, rosemary, savory, thyme.

Mexican Cookery: chili powder, oregano.

Minestrone: basil, oregano.

Mushrooms: mace, nutmeg, tarragon.

Omelets: burnet, caraway, chervil, chives, parsley, sage, savory, tarragon.

Onions: cloves, marjoram, oregano, paprika, sage.

Onion Soup: sage, thyme.

Oriental Cookery: varies depending on national style, but consistently includes ginger, soy sauce; sometimes saffron as well. Chinese cuisine also employs a mixture of herbs and spices, usually including anise, cinnamon, cloves, and fennel; and monosodium glutamate is omnipresent in Chinese dishes. Indonesian cookery also includes the sort of dishes typical of India, such as curries.

Pancakes: cinnamon.

Pastries: anise, cardamom (in Danish pastries).

Peas: marjoram, mint, rosemary, savory, tarragon.

Pea Soup: mint, rosemary, savory.

Pies: allspice, caraway (in crusts).

Pork: anise, caraway, coriander, ginger, grated orange peel, rosemary, sage, savory.

Portuguese Cookery: generally similar to SPANISH COOKERY but using fewer herbs, with most emphasis on such basics as garlic, parsley.

Potatoes: bay leaves, caraway, chives (on baked potatoes with sour cream), dill, mace, paprika, parsley.

Potato Salad: celery seed, dill, fennel, sesame seeds.

Potato Soup: basil, chervil, thyme.

Poultry: see specific kinds.

Puddings: allspice, cinnamon, cloves (usually in combination with cinnamon), nutmeg, grated orange peel, vanilla.

Rice: basil, cumin, curry powder, parsley (as a garnish), saffron, savory, tumeric.

Russian Cookery: bay leaves, dill, some garlic, onions, parsley, peppercorns.

Salads: fresh leafy herbs such as basil, burnet, chervil, chives, marjoram, oregano, sage, tarragon. In fruit salads: mint. In seafood salads: fennel, shallots.

Salad Dressings: chives, garlic, herb vinegars, marjoram, mustard, oregano, paprika, sage.

Sauerkraut: caraway, cumin.

Sausage: coriander, fennel, marjoram.

Scandinavian Cookery: bay leaves, chives, dill, parsley, with a fairly generous use of pepper.

Seafood: cayenne or chili powder (in cocktails), chives, coriander (with shrimp), paprika, saffron, tarragon, thyme, turmeric.

Soups: basil, bay leaves *bouquet garni*, celery seed, chervil, chives (in pale soups), garlic, parsley, saffron (for fish soups), sage, tarragon, thyme. (Also see specific kinds.)

Spaghetti: basil, oregano in traditional sauces. In a butter sauce: parsley.

Spanish Cookery: garlic, parsley, saffron, tarragon, thyme; also some use of cayenne and nutmeg.

Spinach: nutmeg, poppy seeds (in a lemon-butter sauce), rosemary, tarragon.

Squash: cinnamon (with brown sugar), cloves, marjoram, grated orange peel, paprika, rosemary.

Stews: basil, bay leaves, *bouquet garni*, celery seed, cloves, garlic, marjoram, oregano, rosemary, saffron (in fish stews), sage, shallots, thyme.

Stuffings: basil, garlic, marjoram, parsley, sage, shallots, thyme.

Sweet Potatoes: cinnamon (with brown sugar), cloves, grated orange peel.

Syrups: cinnamon, cloves.

Tomatoes: basil, bay leaves, chervil, marjoram, oregano, sage.

Tomato Soup: basil, chervil, sage.

Turkey: basil, marjoram, oregano, thyme.

Veal: rosemary, tarragon.

Vegetables: see specific kinds.

Vegetable Soup: marjoram, parsley, sage, thyme most commonly, but almost any herb(s) of your choice.

Venison: rosemary.

Zucchini: marjoram, oregano.

VII.   All about Weights
and Measures

Accurate measuring is one of the basics—the corollary being that sloppy or inaccurate measuring undoubtedly lies behind many a culinary disaster. Whatever other kitchen equipment you may choose to eschew, measuring implements are, to put it mildly, vital.

You should own at least one or two sets of measuring spoons—tablespoon, teaspoon, and fractions of the latter; a set of measuring cups for dry materials—the kind for which the full measure is the rim of the cup—in full cup, half-cup, one-third-cup, and one-fourth-cup sizes; a one-cup glass measuring cup (and preferably two-cup and four-cup sizes as well) for liquids—the full measure here marked below the rim, with fractional markings below that.

How you use your measuring tools is equally important.

For liquid measuring, it will be helpful to establish a surface in your kitchen that is absolutely level; set your cup there, always, when pouring out liquids, and don't count on your own steadiness of hand. If spoons are involved, bear in mind that the liquid may come a little too fast and dribble over the edge; don't hold the spoon directly above your mixing bowl or cooking container, or you may inadvertently double the amount of the ingredient you intended to include.

Dry measures given in recipes always mean (unless they specify "heaping") leveled-off ones, whether it's cup or spoon you're using; and, except for brown sugar—which should be firmly packed down—the substance should be piled or poured naturally and loosely in your measuring implement. Level off with spoons by using the straight edge of a knife, holding the measuring spoon over your can, box, or bin to catch the excess. To measure out cupfuls, or fractions thereof, set your measure in the center of a sheet of wax paper; pour out the ingredient, letting it spill over; level off, remove the measure, then simply make a trough of the wax paper to slide the leftover back into your keeping-place. Note: unless otherwise specified, flour should be measured after sifting.

Recipes generally use abbreviations for weights and measures. The ones you're most likely to encounter are these:

bu. = bushel

C. = cup (meaning a measuring cup, not a tea or coffee cup)

gal. = gallon

lb. or # = pound(s)

no. or # = number (referring usually to cans, which we'll come to)

oz. = ounce

pk. = peck

pt. = pint

qt. = quart

T. or tbsp. = tablespoon

t. or tsp. = teaspoon

The conflict between # = pounds and # = number is easily resolved. A "2# can of peas" is a 2-pound can, while a "#2 can of peas" is a Number 2 can, which contains considerably less. Simply read the instructions; only one of the two interpretations will make sense.

Measures, rather than weights, will concern you for the

most part—though later in this chapter, you'll find some weight information likely to help in purchasing recipe ingredients. So far as weights go, we shall for purposes of completeness record here the fact that the pound is equal to 16 ounces; the British ounce, should you happen to be using a cookbook published in the United Kingdom, is very slightly different from ours by a fraction of 1 percent, and is for all practical purposes equivalent.

A few Continental European tracts have found their way here as well, and there the metric system is used, based upon grams rather than ounces. To convert grams to ounces, multiply the given number of grams by 0.035 (should you wish to convert in the other direction, the number to use is 28.35). These, to save you the calculation, are some very approximate equivalents:

15 grams - ½ oz.   100 grams - 3½ oz.
30 grams - 1 oz.   500 grams - 17½ oz.
50 grams - 1¾ oz.   1000 grams (also called a
75 grams - 2½ oz.   kilogram) - 35 oz.
                                   (2 lbs. 3 oz.)

Supermarket merchandise tends to be sold by the pound, generally. Some items, though, are not, and you may encounter the following, which (a) are measures, not weights, and (b) have nothing to do with liquid measures by the same names that will be listed later:

1 qt. = 2 pts.
1 pk. = 8 qts.
1 bu. = 8 pks.

Now, to the kitchen, and first, to your **dry measures.**

The following equations will be helpful (of course the weights of these measures will differ for various foods; later in this chapter, some handy approximations):

1 t. = ½ "dessert spoon"   ⅓ C. = 5 T. + 1 t.
1 T. = 3 t.   ½ C. = 8 T.
1½ T. = 1 "heaping" T.   ⅔ C. = ½ C. + 2 T. +
¼ C. = 4 T.   2 t. (or 10 T. + 2 t.)
                            1 C. = 16 T.

For definitions of such nebulous directions as "dash" and "pinch," see Chapter II.

Liquid measures can be a bit more complicated, especially if you find yourself coping with a British cookbook, or one dealing with Continental cuisine. Check, by all means, to see where the book was published—and whether there are any specific explanatory notes—before you begin. If the recipe ingredients are expressed in liters—then the publisher is based in Continental Europe. If cups or pints are used, this is no guarantee that you can use your usual measuring cups—for though Great Britain uses those same designations, they signify radically different quantities from ours. The table on page 136, whether or not you encounter a book published outside the U.S.A., should help you cope.

What has been included in this table, of course, are round numbers, wherever they are likely to occur. Should you be faced with some radically different figures in recipes, get out your slide rule or phone a mathematical friend, and use these formulas:

to convert liters to U.S. quarts: multiply the liters by 1.057;

to convert liters to British quarts: multiply the liters by 0.88;

to convert British quarts to liters: multiply the quarts by 1.14;

Fluid Oz.	American	British	Continental
128	1 gal. = 4 qts. = 16 C.	3.2 qts.	3.785 liters
40	1 qt. + ½ pt.	1 qt. = 2 pts.	1.14 liters
35	1 qt. + ⅓ C. = 4⅓ C.	1¾ pts. = ⅞ qt.	1 liter (10 deciliters)
32	1 qt. = 2 pts. = 4 C.	⅘ qt.	0.95 liter
20	1 pt. + ½ C. = 2½ C.	1 pt. = 2 C. = 4 gills	0.57 liter
17	2 C. + 2 T.	1½ C. + 2 T.	½ liter
16	1 pt. = 2 C. = ½ qt.	⅖ qt.	4.5 deciliters
10	1¼ C.	1 C. = 2 gills = ½ pt.	2.85 deciliters
8	1 C. = ½ pt. = 16 T.	⅖ pt.	2.27 deciliters
5⅓	⅔ C. = ½ C. + 2 T. + 2 t.	½ C. + 1 t.	1.52 deciliters
5	½ C. + 2 T.	1 gill = ¼ pt. = ½ C.	1.42 deciliters
4	½ C. = 8 T. = ¼ pt.	4 T.	1.18 deciliters
3½	6 T. + 2 t.	3½ T.	1 deciliter (0.1 liter)
2⅔	⅓ C. = 5 T. + 1 t.	2 T. + 2 t.	
2	¼ C. = 4 T.	2 T.	
1	2 T. = 6 t. = ⅛ C.	1 T.	
½	1 T. = 3 t.	½ T.	

to convert British quarts to U.S. quarts: multiply the
   British quarts by 1.25;
to convert U.S. quarts to liters: multiply the quarts
   by 0.95;
to convert U.S. quarts to British quarts: multiply the
   U.S. quarts by 0.80.

Most of the measures we've discussed thus far are
volumes—the weights of which, obviously, will differ depending upon the weights of the foods involved. The
following listing will give you a rough—very rough—idea
of the weights or numbers necessary to equal *recipe quantities* of a variety of common ingredients. Do bear in mind
that many of the figures are necessarily approximations;
while it is possible to establish the consistency of, for
example, butter or salt (and the figures there are thus
dependable)—the sizes of such as apples or tomatoes can
vary considerably.

Apples: about 3 average = 1 lb. = about 3 C. chopped.

Apricots, Dried: 1 lb. = about 3 C.

Apricots, Fresh: 9 or 10 average = 1 lb.

Bacon, Raw: 2 oz. = about ⅓ C. diced.

Baking Powder: 1 oz. = 2 T. + 2 t.; 6 oz. = 1 C.

Baking Soda: 1 oz. = 2 to 2½ T.

Beans, Dried: 1 lb. = 2½ C. = 5½ to 6½ C. cooked.

Beans, Snap: 1 lb. = 2½ to 3 C. cooked.

Beets: 1 lb. = about 2 C. diced.

Brussels Sprouts: 1 lb. = 2 to 2½ C. cooked.

Butter or Margarine: 1 lb. = 2 C.; ¼ lb. (1 stick) = 8 T. = ½ C.; 2 oz. = ¼ C.; ½ oz. = 1 T.

Carrots: 1 lb. = 3½ to 4 C. sliced or diced.

Celery: 2 stalks = ¾ to 1 C. sliced.

Cheese, Grated: ¼ lb. = about 1 C.; 1 oz. = about ¼ C.

Chocolate: 1 lb. = 16 squares, enough to dip about 80 candies; 1 square = ¼ C. grated.

Cornmeal: 1 lb. = about 3 C.

Cornstarch: 1 lb. = about 3 C.; 1 oz. = about 4 T.

Cottage Cheese or Cream Cheese: ½ lb. = about 1 C.

Cream, Whipping: 1 C. before whipping = 2 C. whipped.

Eggs: 5 or 6 average = 1 C.; 8 or 9 white = 1 C.; 12 to 14 yolks = 1 C.; 1 egg, lightly beaten = 3 to 4 T. (¼ C. or a little less).

Fat, Solid: see BUTTER.

Flour, All-Purpose: 1 lb., unsifted = about 3½ C.; 1 lb., sifted = about 4 C.; 3½ to 4 oz., sifted = 1 C.

Flour, Cake: 1 lb., sifted = 4½ to 4⅔ C.

Honey: 12 oz. = 1 C.

Lemon Juice: 1 average lemon = 2 T. juice.

Macaroni or Noodles: 1 lb. uncooked = about 8½ C. cooked.

Margarine: see BUTTER.

Meat, Chopped: 1 lb. = about 2 C.

Molasses: 12 oz. = 1 C.

Mushrooms: 1 lb. = 4 to 5 C. sliced or diced.

Noodles: see MACARONI.

Oatmeal: 1 lb. = about 8 C. cooked.

Onions: 1 lb. = 2½ to 3½ C. chopped.

Oranges: 3 average = about 1 lb.

Orange Juice: 1 average orange = 6 to 8 T. juice (up to ½ C.).

Peaches: 4 average = about 1 lb.

Pears: 3 average = about 1 lb.

Peas: 1 lb. = 1 to 1½ C. shelled, depending on size of peas.

Potatoes: 3 or 4 average = about 1 lb.; 1 lb. = 3½ to 4 C. sliced or diced = about 2 C. mashed.

Raisins: 1 lb. = about 3 C.

Rice: ½ lb. raw = about 1 C. = 3 to 3½ C. cooked.

Salt: 1 oz. = 1 T. + 1½ t.

Shallots: 4 average = about ¼ C. minced.

Spaghetti: 1 lb. = about 9 C. cooked.

Spinach: 1 lb. = about 1½ C. cooked.

Sugar, Brown: 1 lb. = 2¼ to 2½ C. (firmly packed, remember).

Sugar, Confectioners':   1 lb. = 3½ to 3¾ C.

Sugar, Granulated: 1 lb. = 2 to 2½ C.

Tomatoes: 3 or 4 average = about 1 lb. = (after peeling, seeding) about 1½ C. pulp.

Turnips: 1 lb. = about 3½ C. sliced.

Walnuts: about 1¼ lbs = 2 C. chopped.

THE CAN CODE

The question of canned foods can be quite confusing, especially if your recipe specifies, say, a "No. 2" can of pineapple juice, or a "Buffet Size" can of tomato sauce— and you find yourself searching your supermarket shelves in vain for such coding. You won't have this trouble with meats, which are simply packaged according to weight— but it's a problem that may crop up with fruits, vegetables, and other foods. The names and numbers are canning-industry designations; sometimes they appear on the cans themselves, and often they don't (though net contents, by law, always do). Those in fairly wide use, with some guidelines regarding their approximate content, are:

Numbers ending in "Z" (with the exception of 6Z and 8Z, discussed separately below) are dependable indications of content in ounces within a fraction of an ounce; they include among standard sizes 4Z, 7Z, 12Z, and 14Z.

The 6Z can is used chiefly for juices and for such substances as tomato paste; its contents can vary from 5 ounces to 6½ ounces—meaning about ¾ cup.

Various 8Z designations are used, each meaning something just a little different; generally speaking, this size can contains anywhere from 7¾ to 9 ounces, approximately 1 cup. The plain "8Z" can comes closest, contains 7¾ to 8 ounces, is used for juices. The contents of the "8Z Tall" can, used chiefly for fruits and vegetables, can cover the full range, from 7¾ ounces of spinach to 9 ounces of figs. "Buffet Size" or "8Z Short" cans are used principally for sauces, and contain 8 to 9 ounces.

Picnic is the designation applied to the can that holds about a 1¼-cup measure. There are two types in this category. "No. 1 Picnic," used mostly for vegetables, contains 10 to 10½ ounces. Just plain "Picnic" is used almost exclusively for condensed soups and contains 10½ to 12 ounces.

The No. 2 Vacuum can holds precisely 12 ounces, or about 1½ cups, of vacuum-pack corn.

No. 211 Cyl. is the industry description of a fruit-juice can containing from 12 to 14 ounces, or 1½ to 1¾ cups.

No. 300 cans are used principally for sauces, soups, and vegetables; they hold from 14 to 16 ounces—1¾ cups or sometimes a little bit more.

The No. 303 can, also called No. 1 Tall, is essentially the 2-cup size, is used for fruits, juices, and vegetables. Contents can vary from 15 ounces, for tomato juice or spinach, to 17 ounces for peaches or potatoes.

No. 3 Vacuum is another special vacuum-pack can, used chiefly for sweet potatoes; it holds 18 ounces, or a little over a pound.

No. 2 designates the 2½-cup-size can, the weight of the contents varying from 18 to 20 ounces; it's used for juices, soups, fruits, some vegetables.

The No. 2½ can, the next standard size, is widely used for fruits and vegetables. Its contents, varying in weight from 27 ounces (for light items like spinach) to 30 ounces (for fruits such as pears and peaches), measure about 3½ cups.

No. 3 Cyl. is another strictly fruit-juice can; it holds 46 ounces, or 5¾ cups.

No. 10 is the giant-size fruit and vegetable can, holding 12 to 13 cups; the weight of the contents can vary, depending on the density of the particular food involved, from 6 pounds to slightly over 7 pounds.

Cans used for fish are in a class—or more accurately several classes—by themselves. The one simply called "Flat" is for shrimp, holds 4½ ounces (drained). Salmon comes in "No. ¼," holding 3 to 4 ounces, and in the "½ lb. Flat," twice the contents of the smaller size. Tuna is also packaged in the "No. ¼" can, as well as in the "No. ½," which holds 6½ to 7 ounces, and the "Family Size," slightly over 9 ounces. Sardines, too, come in a "No. ¼"—though the can's differently shaped—and also in various-shaped "No. 1" cans containing 15 ounces.

VIII. Temperatures and Cooking Times

Strictly speaking, cooking per se is just that: applying a particular degree of heat for a particular amount of time. Sounds more or less mechanical, but don't be deceived: calculating these factors correctly can be something of a fine art.

Temperature is scientifically defined on the basis of water's behavior at precise sea level: it freezes at zero degrees, boils at 100°. Not on your household thermometers, however—nor, for that matter, on any kitchen thermometers you're likely to own; those are points on the Centigrade temperature scale, which is used on the Continent and in scientific laboratories all over, but not in British or American everyday situations. We use the Fahrenheit scale, on which water freezes at 32°, boils at 212° (and, incidentally, simmers at approximately 180° to 185°), and it's degrees Fahrenheit we'll be referring to in this chapter, as well as throughout this book.

Should you encounter a recipe phrased in Continental terms, the following formulas will come in handy: $F = 9/5\ C + 32$ (meaning to convert degrees Centigrade to degrees Fahrenheit, multiply by 9, divide by 5, then add 32); $C = 5/9\ (F-32)$—meaning that to get from Fahrenheit to Centigrade, subtract 32, multiply by 5, and divide that result by 9.

Fat, whether liquid or solid, behaves differently from

143

water, and bubbling does not mean that it is at 212° or any other specific temperature; fat, in fact, is not hot enough to cook in until the bubbling has subsided (calorie counters should know, too, that a too-low cooking temperature means an inordinate amount of the fat will be absorbed by the food). Some examples of proper fat temperatures for frying are 225° for eggs, 275° for pork chops, 325° for hamburgers, 350° for steak, and as a deep-frying minimum, 375° for onions or French-fried potatoes—and you may encounter recipes that spell out the temperatures to use for certain dishes.

The temperature of fat may be taken with a special thermometer, and there are two tests as well. Drop in a few drops of water; if the fat bubbles, it is over 212°—and if it bubbles very actively, it is over 300°. Second test: drop in a small piece of bread, leave it in the fat for exactly 30 seconds, and fish it out; if it is crisp, the temperature of the fat is 350° or more.

The subject of oven temperatures has been complicated by a number of terms that are broadly used, but that rarely mean the same thing from one recipe-writer to another. It is to be fondly hoped that you will be lucky enough to meet only recipes that specify exact numbers of degrees. If, however, you encounter those vague terms, the following rundown of what is usually, or customarily, meant may assist you in making an educated guess as to the writer's intentions.

COOL: about 225°, or lower

WARM or *VERY SLOW:*   250°—but not higher than 275°

SLOW: 275° to 325°

MODERATE: 350° or 375°

MODERATELY HOT: about 400°

HOT: 400° to 450°

VERY HOT: 450° to 500° (or maybe higher)

EXTREMELY HOT: at least 500°

In any case (unless you are putting food into an oven merely to keep it warm—in which case you can turn the oven on when you put the food in), the oven should be at the specified temperature when you insert the food, which means the oven must be preheated. Ovens vary a great deal, and preheating may take anywhere from ten to thirty minutes, depending upon your oven and the aimed-at temperature level. It's a good idea to take two steps: (1) purchase a good-quality oven thermometer, keep it in your oven, and go by the thermometer if there's a difference of opinion between it·and your temperature-control knob; (2) thermometer in place, take half an hour to check just how much time it takes your oven to preheat to various temperatures, and record the results for later time-saving reference (the margins of this page would be a good recording place).

How long you cook a packaged food, and at what temperature, is not normally a problem. Packages usually offer very helpful directions. The common instruction on canned vegetables is "heat"—which means simply put the contents in a saucepan over a flame until the food has become hot. Frozen food packages customarily spell out cooking procedures—which should be followed exactly. Most dry packaged foods such as rice and the various pastas also give specifics, and often include alternatives if the food is to be used as an ingredient in some other dish. Packaged meats, such as tenderized or imported hams, also normally offer cooking advice. Always bear in mind that such advice has been carefully plotted for maximum customer satisfaction, so it's best followed—at least the first time you use the product; if the result is over- or under-cooked for your own taste, you can make adjustments next time (but make notes for future reference).

Chiefly, it's when neither a packaged food nor a recipe is being used that the problems occur—when vegetables are being boiled, or meats roasted, for instance. The list that follows consists chiefly of meats and vegetables, though you will find some other items included (candy, for one, with its esoteric list of special "stage" temperatures). A few things must be borne in mind.

The list concerns chiefly normal top-of-the-stove or oven cookery. If you are using a special device—an electric frying pan, an electric oven, a pressure cooker, a rotisserie—follow the manufacturer's instructions; temperatures and timings may differ from those of usual kitchen appliances.

In roasting meats, a meat-thermometer temperature will sometimes be mentioned; this is a specially designed thermometer for use with meat and poultry, especially handy to have if your oven is somewhat unpredictable. Get one that's top quality. Insert it so it does not touch any bone, and so its tip is in the center of the meat, and not in fat; in poultry, insert it in the fleshy part of the thigh or—if the bird is stuffed—in the stuffing.

The shape of a roast (of any meat) will affect its time in the oven: a long, narrow roast with more surface exposed to the heat will cook faster than a thicker, more compact one—even though they may both weigh exactly the same. If you're roasting meat for guests, incidentally, and you're not quite sure of their arrival time, start early, and take the roast out when you think it's about half an hour short of being done; put it back in the oven when they arrive (at which point, if there's any significant interval, it may need some forty-five minutes, including warming-up-again time).

All the figures in the list that follows are approximations. In addition to the factors noted above, they depend on the condition, quality, and tenderness of the food, your equipment, your personal tastes. If the food in question is chilled, times will be longer than indicated.

Artichokes: Boil 35 to 45 minutes; pressure-cooker time, 10 to 12 minutes.

Asparagus: Boil whole asparagus 10 to 20 minutes; pressure-cooker time, about 1½ minutes. Asparagus tips should be boiled 5 to 10 minutes; pressure-cooker time, about a minute.

Beans, Lima: Boil 15 to 25 minutes; pressure-cooker time, a minute or two.

Beans, Snap: Boil 8 to 15 minutes; pressure-cooker time, 2 to 2½ minutes.

Beef: Roast beef at an oven temperature of 300° to 325°; the timing, depending on how you like your beef and on the shape of the roast, may be from 18 minutes to 40 minutes per pound. Your meat-thermometer reading should be between about 140° (for rare meat) and 170° (well-done).

Broiling or grilling steaks—or other cuts—will of course depend on thickness, distance from the flame, and personal preference. A good-grade steak's broiling time, in your kitchen broiler or on an outside grill, may vary (including cooking both sides) from 8 minutes to 25 minutes. Check frequently during cooking time, to get the steak done to your tastes. The same time spans cover barbecued beef cubes, broiled or grilled hamburgers, and grilled liver.

The average meat loaf is usually baked at an oven temperature of 375° to 425°. Simmering time for beef stews should be, for fully developed flavor, at least two hours and preferably three. Braised beef—pot roast, for example—usually (recipe instructions may vary) takes at least 2½ hours, depending on the weight of the meat.

Beets: Boil small whole beets at least 30 minutes (and up to an hour or more, depending on the age of the beets); pressure-cooker time, 5 to 15 minutes. Sliced or diced beets should be boiled 15 to 20 minutes; pressure-cooker time, 6 to 8 minutes.

Beet Tops: Boil 5 to 15 minutes.

Broccoli: Boil 10 to 15 minutes; pressure-cooker time, 2 to 2½ minutes.

Brussels Sprouts: Boil 10 to 15 minutes; pressure-cooker time, 1 or 2 minutes.

Cabbage: Boil 10 to 15 minutes if quartered, 3 to 10 minutes if shredded; pressure-cooker times are, respectively, 2 or 3 minutes, and approximately 1 minute.

Cakes: Cakes are generally baked at an oven temperature of 300° to 350°—but follow recipe instructions. When the time specified has elapsed (never open the oven to look at a cake until at least half the baking time has passed), test the cake for doneness, these three ways: (1) see if the top surface springs back readily when you press it with a fingertip (not a valid test for chocolate and other very rich cakes, which may not spring back, but may still be done); (2) insert a clean toothpick at center top, and see if it comes out still clean (again, this does not always work with extremely rich cakes); (3) check the sides of the cake, which (in all but sponge-type cakes) should have pulled slightly away from the sides of the pan.

Candy: In candy-making, as in the concoction of some

other sweet things such as frostings, you are often asked to determine the temperature stage which a syrupy mixture has achieved; such stages are very specifically defined— well, not always specifically, but certainly more so than, for example, oven temperatures, discussed at the beginning of this chapter. The temperatures, at any rate, can be easily determined by the use of a candy thermometer designed specifically for this purpose; as a double check, the temperature can be determined by dropping a bit of the syrup into cold water, and your recipe may so specify. (Whether by thermometer or cold-water testing, the mixture in question should be removed from heat for the purpose, since the temperature can increase rather swiftly even while testing is taking place.) The important temperature stages most mentioned in recipes, and the action of the bit of syrup when dropped into the cold water, are:

RIBBON STAGE: 230°- 234°—syrup forms soft ribbon.

SOFT BALL STAGE: 234°- 238°—syrup forms soft ball which, when taken out of the water, collapses.

HARD BALL STAGE: reached from about 250° to 265° (varies), and sometimes subclassified as "firm" (the ball holds its shape when removed from the water but is still malleable) and "hard" (the ball can actually be clinked against a hard surface). The "firm" point is the final one for taffies.

CRACK STAGE: approximately 270° to 290° (again, it may vary)—syrup separates into thin strands that are harder as the temperature increases, but not brittle.

HARD CRACK STAGE: 300°-310°—the thin strands are definitely brittle (this is the final stage for brittles and hard candies).

(Also see CHOCOLATE-DIPPING.)

Carrots: Boil 15 to 30 minutes whole (depending on size and age), 10 to 20 minutes if sliced; pressure-cooker times are, respectively, 3 to 12 minutes and 1½ to 2 minutes.

Cauliflower: Boil 15 to 25 minutes whole, 8 to 10 minutes if separated; corresponding pressure-cooker times are 10 minutes and 2 to 3 minutes.

Celery: Boil cut-up celery about 15 minutes; pressure-cooker time, 2 or 3 minutes.

Chard: Boil 10 to 20 minutes; pressure-cooker time, 2 or 3 minutes.

Chicken: Roast chicken at an oven temperature of 350°, a little lower if you use a covered roasting pan; the time required may vary from 20 or 30 minutes per pound for an unstuffed bird to 35 or 40 minutes per pound if the chicken is stuffed. The chicken is done when the leg joints are freely movable, and when your meat thermometer inserted in the thigh reads 180° to 190° (about 175° if inserted in the stuffing).

Broiling or grilling chicken, as with meats, may take varying lengths of time depending on the size of the pieces (barbecuing a whole bird will of course take longer), distance from the flames, and so on. Chicken fricassee needs from 40 to 90 minutes of simmering, depending on the age of the bird; older, tougher ones take longest.

Chocolate-Dipping: A couple of special tips, here, for making chocolate candies. Keep your melted chocolate (melted over hot water in a double boiler) between 85° and 110° while you're doing the dipping—and keep your room temperature below 65°.

Clams: Steaming clams (with half a cup of boiling water to each two dozen clams) takes from 15 to 20 minutes till the shells open. Baking requires about 5 or 10 minutes at an oven temperature of 425°.

Collards: Boil 10 to 20 minutes.

Corn: Boil 5 to 15 minutes; pressure-cooker time, 1 minute to a minute and a half. Grilling corn, as you might for a barbecue, generally takes 15 to 20 minutes.

Crabs: Boiling, starting with live ones, takes about 20 minutes.

Dandelion Greens: Boil 10 to 20 minutes.

Duck: Duck, like chicken, should be roasted at an oven temperature of 350° or a little lower; time ranges from about 20 minutes per pound for an unstuffed bird to 30 or 35 minutes per pound for a stuffed one. Doneness criteria for CHICKEN apply.

Eggplant: Boil sliced eggplant for 10 to 20 minutes.

Fish: Baking a whole fish, at an oven temperature of 400° to 425°, takes about 10 minutes per pound, up to 15 or 20 minutes per pound if the fish is stuffed. Broiled or grilled fillets usually take 5 to 10 minutes, depending on their thickness and the distance from the flames; steaks similarly cooked normally take a little bit longer, up to 15 minutes.

Frostings: Recipes often refer to mysterious "soft ball" and other temperature stages; see CANDY.

Goose: Roast a goose at about the same oven temperature as you would a chicken or duck, about 350°; roasting time varies from 15 to 35 minutes per pound—depending on the size of the bird (a larger bird means fewer minutes per pound) and whether or not it is stuffed (stuffing increases the time slightly). See CHICKEN for doneness indications; they apply here as well.

Ham: Bake ham at an oven temperature of 300°, or at most 325°; time required, depending chiefly on the shape of the ham, will generally range from 18 to 30 minutes per pound. The final reading on your meat thermometer should be between 160° and 170°.

Kale: Boil 15 to 25 minutes.

Lamb: A lamb roast is best started at an oven temperature of 450°, with the temperature reduced to 350° after 15 minutes; total time (including that first 15 minutes) ranges—depending on the shape of the roast and your own preferences—from about 15 minutes per pound for a roast with bone to 30 or 35 minutes per pound for a boned-and-rolled roast. Your meat-thermometer reading—again depending on your own preferences—should be 165° or 170° for a well-done roast, 150° or 155° for one that is done to a medium turn.

Broiling or grilling, as with any meat, depends as to time on size and thickness of cuts, distance from the flames, and so on. Chops may take from 12 or 15 minutes up to 20 or 25, depending on the foregoing factors. Cubed and marinated lamb, often an ingredient of shish kebab, may take some 20 minutes on a skewer over a flame.

Lamb stew should be simmered at least two hours. Braised-lamb dishes (follow your particular recipe) generally require about an hour and a half.

Lobster: Live lobsters need about 5 minutes per pound of boiling—a total of 10 minutes for the most flavorful size. Broiling or grilling generally takes some 15 to 20 minutes.

Okra: Boil for 10 to 15 minutes; pressure-cooker time, 3 or 4 minutes.

Onions: Boil for 15 to 30 minutes, depending upon the size of the onions and your cooking purposes; pressure-cooker time, 3 to 7 minutes. Onions skewered for barbecuing will cook, depending on size and distance from the flame, in 8 to 12 minutes.

Parsnips: Boil whole parsnips 20 to 35 minutes, quartered ones 10 to 20 minutes; pressure-cooker times are, respectively, 8 to 10 minutes and 4 to 7 minutes.

Peas: Boil 8 to 10 minutes; pressure-cooker time, a minute or less.

Pork: There is no need to overcook pork; trichinosis organisms are killed well under the well-done stage. Roast pork at 325° to 350°; the time required is 30 to 45 minutes per pound (more time if the roast has been boned), and your meat-thermometer reading should be 180° to 185°.

Pork cuts, such as chops or spare ribs, generously basted or pre-marinated, usually take about 35 or 40 minutes to grill or barbecue. Braised-pork dishes (follow your recipe, of course) normally take about an hour.

Potatoes: Boil for 25 or 30 minutes if whole (medium size), about 20 minutes if quartered or cut into large pieces, about 10 or 15 minutes if diced or cut into small pieces; pressure-cooker times are 8 to 10 minutes for whole potatoes, 5 minutes or less for cut-up ones.

It takes about an hour (or sometimes less—test for tenderness by poking with a fork) to bake potatoes, at 450° to 500° oven temperature, or to grill them.

Rutabagas: Boil them, cut up, 20 to 30 minutes; pressure-cooker time, 6 to 8 minutes.

Shrimp: Boil fresh shrimp about 5 minutes. Precooked shrimp being broiled or grilled take about 1 to 3 minutes if shelled, 2 to 4 minutes if in their shells.

Spinach: Cook for 3 to 8 minutes (not boiling, but wetting the leaves and adding no other water); pressure-cooker time, usually less than a minute.

Squash: Boil the summer type, sliced, 10 to 20 minutes; pressure-cooker time, 2 or 3 minutes. Boil the winter type, cut up, 15 to 25 minutes; pressure-cooker time, 5 to 10 minutes.

Sweet Potatoes: Boil 25 to 30 minutes; pressure-cooker time, 5 to 7 minutes.

Tomatoes: Boil them, cut in quarters, 7 to 10 minutes; pressure-cooker time, a minute or less. Skewered for shish kebab, they'll be done in 2 or 3 minutes.

Turkey: Choose turkey-roasting temperature on the basis of poundage. Turkeys up to 14 pounds should be roasted at an oven temperature of 325°, and will take from 18 to 35 minutes per pound (a stuffed bird will take about five minutes more than that per pound). Turkeys over 14 pounds should be roasted at 300°, and will take some 13 to 18 minutes per pound (again, a stuffed bird will take longer). The doneness tests for CHICKEN prevail here as well, and there is a "prediction test" you can make with turkey: before you roast the turkey, simmer the gizzard until it is tender when pierced with a fork; note the time that took to achieve, add one hour, and the result is the probable roasting time for the whole turkey.

Turnips: Boil whole turnips 20 to 30 minutes, cut-up ones 10 to 15 minutes; corresponding pressure-cooker times are 9 to 12 minutes and 1 to 1½ minutes.

Turnip Greens: Boil 10 to 25 minutes.

Veal: Roast veal at an oven temperature of 300°, and figure the time at 25 to 45 minutes per pound, depending upon the shape of the roast; your meat-thermometer reading should be about 170°.

Usual braised-veal dishes take from 45 to 90 minutes, but follow the specific recipe instructions. Veal stew should be simmered at least two hours.

IX. How Many for Dinner?

Purchasing and preparing just the right amount of something for the number of people involved doesn't usually pose much of a problem for the cook who's been at it for a number of years; experience, here, is an excellent teacher.

The novice, though, can understandably be at a loss. How large a roast is needed to serve family plus dinner guests? How many pounds of carrots, or spinach? Even the old kitchen hand can be brought up short. How much butter's needed to spread enough slices to make sandwiches for two troops of scouts? How much potato salad to serve a church supper for fifty? How much ice cream?

The listing in this chapter answers those questions, as well as a number of other quantity dilemmas. Bear in mind, of course, that they are rough estimates only; your family, or your dinner guests, may eat more or less than these "average" portions, and the quantity of one menu item will of course be affected by what you're serving with it, how many courses there are, and so on (serving a huge plate of soup first, for instance, will cut main-course appetites). Figures here are for adults; children's appetites vary considerably, and can be quite unpredictable unless you're familiar with the youngsters involved.

As a general rule, it's better to err on the side of too much (leftovers can always be used for something) than too little. And bear in mind, too, that appetites tend to be bigger out-of-doors; increase amounts a little for picnics or barbecues.

Remember to refer to Chapters III and IV, to be sure of quality as well as quantity, and if you're using canned food, turn to Chapter VII for the rundown on can sizes and contents. Also rely, when you're shopping, on the guidance of butchers and other food-store people; their advice here, as on many things, can often be very helpful.

One warning: beware of recipe-writers who tend to overestimate the number of mouths their concoctions will feed. Not all of them do it, of course, but there's enough of that kind of wishful thinking that it's well to be on the alert, especially when you first open a particular cookbook; once you're familiar with the author's tendencies in this area, there's less of a problem.

Asparagus: Plan on serving 6 to 8 stalks to each person.

Bacon: There are usually about a dozen slices in a half-pound package; the customary serving (as, with eggs): 3 or 4 slices.

Beans, Lima: Buy about ¾ pound (in pods) per person.

Beans, Snap: Figure ⅓ to ½ pound per person.

Beef, Braised or Stewed: Allow ½ pound per person. (Also see HAMBURGER; ROASTS; STEAK.)

Broccoli: The usual serving is about 3 stalks.

Brussels Sprouts: Buy ¼ to ⅓ pound per person; a

quart (they're often sold that way) comes to about 1¼ pounds, will serve four or five.

Butter: A pound will spread from 60 to 80 slices of bread—the same number of sandwiches if you spread only 1 slice, half that number if you butter both slices; whipped butter goes a little further.

Carrots: About ⅓ pound per person is normally adequate; for church-supper planning, figure 15 or 16 pounds for each fifty people.

Cauliflower: Buy about ⅓ pound per person—meaning a cauliflower about 8 inches across will serve from four to six.

Chard: Buy about ¼ pound per person.

Chicken: If broiled, fried, or roasted, plan on a pound— more or less—per person, depending on the rest of the menu; if you're barbecuing, figure that each adult will eat half of a fairly small bird. For stewing chicken, figure about ¾ pound per person.

Clams: For the appetizer kind, figure 6 per person; for steamers, figure at least 15 or 20 for each diner.

Coffee: A pound makes 35 to 40 cups, depending on strength and method used.

Collards: Average serving is about ⅓ pound.

Corn on the Cob: Allow 1 or 2 ears per person, definitely the latter if the cooking is being done outdoors.

Crab, Soft-Shell: For the usual Atlantic types, figure on

2 per person; the Pacific kinds run a little larger, and 1 per person may be enough.

Duck: Plan on a full pound, or perhaps a little more, per person.

Eggplant: The usual serving is about ¼ pound.

Fish: For fillets or steaks, almost or entirely boneless, allow ½ pound per person; when serving fish whole, figure up to a full pound for each diner; a serving of fish sticks is usually 8 or 10 sticks.

Frankfurters: Depending on the dish, plan on 2 or more franks per serving; a packaged pound, which usually contains 10 franks, will thus serve at least four, maybe five.

Goose: Calculate roast-goose weight at a pound per person.

Ham: Whether baked ham or ham steaks, ⅓ to ½ pound is a good-sized serving.

Hamburger: Half a pound makes 2 patties, the usual serving; the patties can be enlarged via extenders such as egg, crumbs, minced onions, et al.

Ice Cream: Count on about 5 servings per quart; for a large gathering of, say, fifty people, you'd need about 10 quarts.

Lamb: For chops, figure 2 per person; roast lamb will serve two people per pound if it's been boned, two people for each 1½ to 2 pounds if the bone's included; when buying lamb for stew, allot about ¾ pound per person.

Lettuce: If you're tossing salad for a big crowd, buy 4 or 5 heads of lettuce for each twenty-five people.

Liver: One pound will usually serve three or four people.

Lobster: Figure on 1 per person, unless the lobsters are unusually large—then a bit less, perhaps only half a lobster, for each diner; for lobster tails alone, allot 2 per person if they're quite large, 3 or 4 if they're small.

Mushrooms: A pound will usually serve two people if the mushrooms are used as a regular vegetable, more if they're just a garnish or part of a sauce or gravy.

Onions: Plan, when serving them—such as the small white "boilers"—as a vegetable, on ¼ to ⅓ pound per person.

Oysters: However you prepare them, whether raw or cooked, 6 or 8 per person is the usual.

Parsnips: The average serving comes to about ⅓ pound.

Peas: Buy ½ pound (in the pod) per person; shelled, 2 cups will serve three or four, depending on the rest of the menu.

Pie: A 10-inch pie serves, with average portions, six people.

Pork: Plan on 2 chops per person; in dishes using pork loin, allow about ⅔ pound per person. (Also see SPARE RIBS.)

Potatoes: Depending on size of the potatoes, figure on 1 to 3 per person in boiling them, mashing them, or in casserole dishes; if cooking for a crowd, a peck of potatoes (about 60 pounds) will serve about fifty people with mashed potatoes. Baking potatoes should be figured at 1 per person.

Potato Salad: A quart will serve about five people.

Rice: If it's part of the main dish, measure out ½ cup (before cooking) for each diner; about half that amount will be needed if the rice is being served as a simple vegetable or side dish.

Roasts: If the roast is boneless, each pound will usually serve two people; if there's bone included, figure a pound per person.

Sausage: For patties, allow ¼ to ⅓ pound per serving; for link sausage, plan on 5 or 6 links for each person.

Scallops: Half a pound per person is the average serving.

Shrimp: As part of a main dish, allow half a pound per person; served as an appetizer, count on ¼ pound, or a little less, for each serving.

Soup: In planning for a large crowd, figure that you'll need 6 quarts (a gallon and a half) for each twenty-five people.

Spaghetti: If it's your main dish, figure 4—or at the most, 5—servings from each 1-pound box; as a side dish, you'll serve double that number.

Spare Ribs: Allow about 1 pound per person.

Spinach: Buy ⅓ to ½ pound per person (i.e., each pound serves two or three).

Squash: Buy ⅓ to ½ pound per person.

Steak: Make ½ to ¾ pound per person as a rule; for outdoor grilling, figure on more, up to a pound per person.

Stew Meat: Requirements will vary, depending a great deal on the number and quantity of other ingredients, but for a good, meaty stew, figure on ½ pound per person if the meat is boneless, about ¾ pound per person if bones are included.

Sweetbreads: You'll need ¼ to ⅓ pound per person.

Tomatoes: Sliced or stuffed, figure 1 whole tomato per serving.

Turkey: Allow ¾ to 1 pound per person; thus, a 10-pound bird will usually last a family of five for two days, with leftover meat used for nibbles, sandwiches, or hash on the second day.

Turnips: Plan on ¼ to ⅓ pound per serving.

Veal: For chops, buy 2 per person; ½ pound of scallops (for such dishes as Veal Parmigiana), or perhaps a bit less, constitutes 1 serving; roast leg, shoulder, or breast serves four to six for each 3 pounds (½ to ¾ pound per person).

Vegetables: A package of frozen vegetables generally serves three people. If you want to use only part of a solidly frozen package, you can cut right through it with a meat saw or with a knife that's been dipped in hot water, returning the remaining part to the freezer after adding foil or plastic wrapping. Some frozen vegetables now come, too, in plastic bags designed to let you spill out just the amount you need; the bag is then rolled down, taped or held with a rubber band, and returned to the freezer. If you're serving canned vegetables to a large crowd, get about three No. 10 cans for each fifty people. Fresh vegetables: see individual listings.

X. Substitutes and Stand-ins

The ideal way to reproduce a dish, of course, is to follow the recipe precisely—ingredient for ingredient, amount for amount. But there are times when that's impractical or impossible: when you're fresh out of the called-for item, for example, or if you must consider the needs of a restricted diet. Too, there may be leftovers you'd like to use up in some sensible way.

Main ingredients, naturally, can't be changed without creating a totally different dish. Minor ones, though, often can be, especially if they're meant merely to play a part in preparation and not to be clearly identified at the dinner table.

Items in the listing that follows are the ones you'll find in your recipes; with each, one or more replacements that will work reasonably well under the given circumstances. Do bear in mind, however, that there will be certain flavor alterations—margarine, for example, does *not* taste "exactly like the high-priced spread," no matter what its makers may claim—and that's something you must take into account. Though there's another side to that particular coin: a taste change may sometimes enhance the dish, or at the least bring welcome variation to a frequent and familiar menu item (case in point: replacing water in a gelatin mix with fruit juice).

Bread Crumbs: an equal amount of crushed cornflakes or other cold cereal, tossed in a little melted butter, if you wish, to soften them.

Butter: margarine, in almost any context, used in the same amount. Also, in baking, the same amount of solid vegetable shortening, combined with ½ teaspoon of salt per cup.

Butter, Melted: see SHORTENING, MELTED.

Buttermilk: see SOUR MILK.

Cake Flour: sifted all-purpose flour—but use just ⅞ cup for each 1 cup of cake flour specified.

Chocolate: cocoa; use 3 tablespoons, plus 1 tablespoon of fat, for each square (or ounce) of chocolate specified.

Coffee, Strong Black: an equal quantity of instant coffee, made double-strength.

Cream: an equal amount of evaporated milk, undiluted.

Eggs: in baking or when used for thickening, 2 egg yolks replacing each whole egg specified. (You may have yolks left over after making, say, a meringue that calls for the use of whites only; see Chapter V for hints on keeping them.)

Flour for Thickening: ½ tablespoon of cornstarch, or ½ tablespoon of arrowroot starch, or 2 teaspoons of quick-cooking tapioca—each, a substitute for 1 tablespoon of flour. (Also see CAKE FLOUR.)

Herbs and Spices: many possible substitutions; among

commonly employed interchangeables are rosemary and sage, turmeric and saffron, oregano and basil, nutmeg and mace. See Chapter VI, Part 2, for many specific suggestions.

Honey: an equal quantity of molasses; or, 1 cup of sugar plus ¼ cup water or other liquid for each specified cup of honey.

Lemon Juice, Fresh: reconstituted lemon juice, 2 tablespoons for each to-be-squeezed lemon specified.

Milk: evaporated milk, ½ cup combined with ½ cup of water (for use in baking make those ⅓ cup and ⅔ cup), for each cup of milk specified; or, an equal quantity of reconstituted nonfat dry milk, combined with 2½ teaspoons of butter or margarine per cup. Also, in a prepared cake-frosting mix, an equal amount of cream (the frosting will of course be richer).

Molasses: an equal quantity of honey.

Seasonings: see Chapter VI.

Shallots: see Chapter VI, Part 1.

Shortening, Melted: an equal quantity of salad oil. This substitution applies only in cooking, of course, not when melted butter, say, is to be used as a dip for seafood or as a serving addition to cooked vegetables.

Skim Milk: an equal amount of reconstituted nonfat dry milk.

Sour Milk or Buttermilk: an equal quantity of sweet or evaporated milk combined with 1 tablespoon of lemon juice or vinegar per cup.

Spices: see HERBS AND SPICES.

Stock (Meat): bouillon cubes or concentrate combined with hot water in the specified amount; also, canned broth or bouillon.

Sugar: brown sugar, in instances where the flavor change is desirable. In desserts or in tea, honey or jam. In instances where a cut in calories or sweets is desired, and only the sweet taste (not texture) is important: nonsugar artificial sweetener (follow bottle directions to calculate equivalent amount).

Vinegar: an equal amount of dry wine, or an equal amount of lemon juice.

Water: any other free-flowing liquid with appropriate flavor, e.g.: vegetable juice or broth in stews, in sauces, as a cooking medium; fruit juice in gelatin; fruit juice, or half-and-half water and fruit juice, in cake-frosting mixes.

Whipped Cream: as a dessert topping, slightly sweetened sour cream.

XI. Tools of the Trade

Your tools of the culinary trade can be as simple or complex, as plain or as fancy, as few or as numerous as you wish. It's possible to get by with very little in the way of cooking utensils and devices, especially if you're cooking for just one or two—and it's certainly silly to crowd your kitchen with useless dust-catchers. There are, on the other hand, many things that can save you time and trouble, and are wise buys for that reason. By and large, you'll do best to buy new utensils and equipment gradually, gearing your kitchen collection to your own cooking needs—the size of your family, the frequency and kind of entertaining you do, the dishes you make most often—and to your personal preferences.

In this chapter, a potpourri of items together with the author's comments (impersonal or otherwise) and, in some cases, care-and-cleaning tips. Speaking of the latter, it's always smart to keep any little leaflets or instruction cards that come with cooking utensils or electric appliances; file them in a drawer or some other catch-all (the author finds the pocket in the back of a looseleaf recipe book handy). That way you'll know for sure if the coffee pot's immersible, whether or not it's wise to use a scouring pad on a particular baking dish, how long to preheat the electric oven, and so on—things it's best not to trust to memory.

Before the list begins, some general cleaning tips (in no particular order) that may come in handy: The sooner you wash a cooking utensil, the easier it is to get the thing clean; try, if you can, to wash utensils during cooking, perhaps while something else is boiling, simmering, or browning—but if you can't, do soak it in hot suds, to save backbreaking scouring later. Anything that gets scorched, with cooked-on food, is best soaked overnight. Non-kitchen gadgets can be useful in the kitchen: pipe cleaners to clean narrow things such as coffeepot spouts, for example, and detergent-dipped cotton swabs to get to hard-to-reach places.

To brighten darkened aluminum utensils, try rubbing with a little lemon juice before washing. Attack stains on "stainless" steel by wetting your scouring pad with a weak ammonia solution instead of just plain water. And baking soda is an effective polishing agent for chrome (use it dry; do the polishing with a soft cloth).

Baking Dishes: These shallow, open dishes come in a variety of sizes and materials, and in shapes running from round to oval or rectangular; they are usually meant for serving as well as cooking in. Smaller sizes are good for many baking uses and *au gratin* dishes; larger sizes can double as roasting pans. One of the larger enameled-metal or glass baking dishes is a must for Italian dishes such as lasagne. If you use a baking dish only occasionally, you might invest in one of the temperature-resistant ceramic types with separate cover and detachable handle that can act as baking dish, casserole, or frying pan.

Baking Sheets: You'll really need 1 or 2 baking sheets only if you plan much cooky- or candy-making; otherwise, aluminum foil folded to double or triple thickness for rigidity can be a workable substitute.

Baster: If you do a good deal of poultry roasting, or any other cooking where basting's required and the liquid involved is shallow and hard to spoon up, the bulb type of baster—a long glass, metal, or plastic tube with a rubber bulb at one end, rather like a giant syringe—is a mighty handy thing to have. It's also good for removing things, as grease from the surface of a simmering liquid.

Blender: You can get along for ages without a blender, though cooks who own them often wonder how they ever did. A blender, these days, cannot only blend, but can mix, purée, chop, grate, and do all kinds of other things that can get pretty tedious the old by-hand way; additionally, there are many newly devised recipes—notably soups and beverages of many sorts—that are virtually impossible to carry out by any other method. Our advice: Get familiar with culinary basics, first; then, put a blender on the list submitted to your particular Santa Claus.

Bottles: Save the quart-size ones with screw tops that come with fruit juices and other things; they're handy for keeping stock, soup, and similar liquids, and also good to have around when you get home from the grocery with a leaky milk carton. If you have trouble cleaning out a narrow-necked bottle, try a vinegar-and-hot-water solution—or drop in a handful of crushed eggshells to act as an abrasive.

Bowls: Have them in several sizes for the mixing that's required in practically every recipe—very small ones for lightly beating a single egg, quite large ones for such procedures as putting together meat loaf ingredients. The colorful ceramic kind are the most attractive, but also breakable; stainless steel is a bit more practical. Devotees of French cuisine favor round-bottomed copper bowls for the beating of egg whites, and somehow eggs do seem to whip up better that way, but such bowls are hard to find.

Broiling Pans: Unless you enjoy scouring your oven's broiling rack and drip pan, the disposable corrugated-aluminum broiling pans widely available in supermarkets are well worth the price; they're also good for baking such things as crumb-coated cut-up chicken, where there's no sauce involved and you want the extra fat to drain off.

Broiling Rack: We refer, here, to the long-handled rack into which you can clamp franks, steaks, or other meats for cooking over a grill or barbecue pit; the meat's held firmly between two metal grids, can be quickly and easily flipped over when one side's done (and the rack's pick-up-able to check cooking progress as well). An inexpensive outdoor-cookery item, worth having.

Cake Pans: The size and kind you should buy depend on the sort of baking you'll be doing. Basic shapes are round and square, in 8-, 9- or 10-inch dimensions; an 8-inch square pan is roughly equivalent in content to a 9-inch round one, a 9-inch square one to a 10-inch round one. If you plan angel food or sponge cakes, you'll need tube pans—round, deep, with a hollow tube at the center—as well.

Cake Racks: These are simple metal racks with small legs at the corners, for cooling cakes—or, for that matter, anything else—so air can circulate underneath as well as above and around. Get them to fit your pot-roast pot and your roasting pan, and they'll then play both roles.

Can Opener: There are both mechanical and electric ones; if you buy the former, at least get the newer type that makes its way around the can by means of a little lever you turn, not by sheer muscle. Electric can openers make the job quick and easy; some include accessories such as knife sharpeners as well. Caution: watch what you're buying, and make sure that all kinds of cans can be accommodated; some electric openers work only with standard round cans.

Canisters: Every kitchen needs some (or giant-size screw-top jars, which aren't as attractive) for such things as flour, sugar, and such; the small ones are good for storing herbs and spices. Be sure the tops fit tightly; the whole point of a canister is keeping the contents from air and from acquiring (or losing) moisture.

Carving Board: This grooved wooden board is meant for cutting roasts and poultry without making a mess; juices run into the shallow troughs and into a little well at one end. Carving boards come in various sizes to accommodate things from small roasts up to big turkeys; the larger sizes often have prongs to hold the food in place while you're carving. Be sure to buy the size that suits your own needs.

Casseroles: For stews, for other one-dish meals, for multiple baked-dish needs, it's good to own a number of casseroles in a variety of sizes; they range from a quart or 2 up to 8 or 10 quarts, but unless you have a large family (or large numbers of dinner guests) you won't need any larger than 5 or 6 quarts. Temperature-resistant ceramic ones are good (though breakable); cast iron, or enameled cast iron, is even better for sturdiness and for good conduction and distribution of heat over long cooking periods. Both these types will go from refrigerator to oven without cracking, and are usually designed for attractive serving as well.

Chafing Dishes: It makes sense to buy these food-keeper-warmers only if you do the kind of entertaining for which they'd be genuinely useful: buffet suppers involving hot dishes, must-be-hot concoctions such as fondues, and the like. Some chafing dishes are electrically operated, others use warming candles or canned heat.

Coffee Maker: The way you make your coffee is entirely a matter of personal preference. Many people, including the author, swear by the filter method that puts the coffee through special filter paper inserted in a beaker-shaped glass server; others like coffee made by perking, dripping, or vacuum devices. It's wise to sample a number of systems, and to ask hostesses how they've done it when you taste coffee you especially like. Electric percolators are of course extremely convenient: they'll keep coffee at drinking temperature over a period of time, can be set (by plugging into a timer or electric clock) to turn themselves on at prearranged times. There are some disadvantages to the electric types, though. Most are not fully immersible in water (though some are, and accompanying literature will so state), thus can't be as thoroughly cleaned; that kind should have soapy water perked through for fifteen or twenty minutes periodically. Some seem to give the coffee a metallic taste. And of course something can always go wrong with the heating element, and frequently does; though replacement is (in large cities, at least) easy and inexpensive, that doesn't help for immediate use, and if you use an electric, it's wise to have a spare stove-top percolator for emergencies.

Colander: This perforated metal bowl, usually with both handles and small legs, is a kitchen basic, useful for draining just about anything that needs draining from spaghetti to canned fruits to just-washed lettuce. Be sure to wash it thoroughly after each use, so the holes don't get plugged up.

Cookbooks: A less-mess tip here: when you're following a recipe, slip your open cookbook into a plastic bag, or enclose it in plastic wrap, to protect the pages from accidental splatters and spills.

Custard Dishes: Get the kind made of heat-resistant glass; they're suitable not only for baking custards, but also for puddings and fruit gelatins, since each holds just about a half-cup portion (the usual package of these desserts makes 4 such portions).

Cutting (and Chopping) Board: A basic need, for otherwise you're likely to ruin table- or counter-tops (or your knives); cutting boards are made of hardwood resilient enough not to dull your knives, but strong enough to stand up under the strain. If you're just setting up housekeeping, you might consider a whole counter-top or work table made of this (or even, if you've quite a large kitchen, a separate butcher block); big chunks of it are available through restaurant- and butcher-supply dealers. Be sure to clean your cutting board or area after each use, so odors don't linger and affect other foods; and if you rub it with linseed oil at the very start, it will help to keep things from penetrating.

Dishwasher: If you've a large family, hence many dishes to wash, a dishwasher is a worthwhile time- and work-saver and a sensible investment. As with all appliances, especially electrical ones, be sure to follow the manufacturer's instructions faithfully; don't overload the washer, do use the specified kind and quantity of detergent, and so on. Find out, when you buy a washer or other major appliance, about service procedures and guarantees, and don't forget to mail in the maker's warranty card.

Double Boiler: Once a must for cereal-making, the double boiler still—in these days of palatable instant oatmeal —fills a useful role in heating anything that shouldn't be placed over direct heat, as melting chocolate for candy or frosting, or reheating leftover rice and other liquidless things.

Eggbeater: Purists use a whisk for eggs themselves, but whether you do or not, you'll need a beater for batters, whipping cream, mousses, and the like. The familiar hand-held rotary beater works fine, but takes longer than an electric mixer-beater. There are two basic types of the latter: the kind that stands on your counter and usually comes with its own bowl, and the hand-held kind that hangs on the wall when not in use. Space and your own preference should be your guide; if you buy the hand-held type, be sure to heft several before buying, get one you're comfortable with. Clean stubborn, sticky food from beater blades by beating in a bowl of detergent suds.

Flour Sifter: This clever device puts the flour through several layers of screening, a procedure that must—as noted in Chapter VII—precede measuring. Be sure to have a sifter, if you do any baking at all. After washing it, let it air-dry, and be sure it's thoroughly dry before putting it away; some cooks, not including the author, avoid the whole problem by storing the sifter in a securely tied plastic bag, and never washing it at all.

Food Chopper: You may or may not need one, depending on how much chopping of what kinds of things you do, as well as your choice of methods. One kind of chopper, good for vegetables, is simply a bowl accompanied by a big curved blade with a handle in the middle; vegetables may also be chopped with a knife on a cutting board, of course. Another kind of chopper is a glass jar with a tall, spring-operated knob in the center of its lid; attached to that shaft are several sharp blades, and plunging the knob up and down brings the blades down on the jar's contents. This kind of chopper is very good for small items such as nuts, shallots, garlic cloves, and in the author's view a handy kind to have; some cooks prefer to crush nuts, wrapped in wax paper, with a rolling pin, and it's up to you. And some blenders can perform some chopping chores, too.

Forks: The kind that come with cooking-utensil sets do things that, in the author's view, are better accomplished by tongs. You will need one to hold things being carved, and one usually comes with a carving knife. If you do outdoor cooking, have an extra-long-handled one (sometimes called a "barbecue fork"). And wooden ones— available as part of salad-serving sets—are good for stirring things, such as rice, where a fork is preferable to a spoon.

Freezer: See REFRIGERATOR-FREEZER.

Frying Basket: It's not really important to have one unless you do deep-frying; though it's good, too, for fishing small vegetables—such as snap beans—as well as corn on the cob out of a deep kettle of water (but you can of course use sieve or colander or—for corn—a pair of tongs for the purpose).

Frying Pans: Like saucepans, frying pans or skillets are among your most basic kitchen basics. Start with at least two sizes—cast iron is a good material for the larger one—and add others as you see the need for them. Teflon-coated ones need little or no oil, but good care to preserve the finish. If you do a good deal of frying, as opposed to simple browning or sautéing, you might want to invest in an electric frying pan that lets you figure temperature and time precisely, and can be used for table-top cookery (it's perfect for sukiyaki, for one thing).

Funnel: This is one of those cheap little things it's just nice to have around because it's bound to come in handy sooner or later. As, when you want to pour something into a bottle with a narrow neck. It's also a way to separate eggs, if you find yourself fumbling with the usual method of flipping the yolk back and forth between half shells; use a fairly small funnel over a glass or jar, break the egg into it, and the yolk will be held while the white slides through.

Garbage Container: You need one, of course, and it should have a lid to keep odors in, insects out. The most convenient kind is the one with the lid that pops up when you depress a foot pedal—leaves both hands free. Clean it often, keep a deodorant cake in it, and line it with a leakproof plastic bag for easy disposal.

Garlic Press: This is a simple mechanical device into which you insert a clove or two of garlic; you can thus mix the resultant juicy pulp with whatever you're cooking, avoiding the sometimes unpleasant shock of biting down on a piece of the pure chopped stuff. If you're a frequent user of garlic, whether in cooked dishes or salads, this is a good thing to have.

Gloves, Rubber: Have a pair on hand. Good, sturdy ones with nonslip fingertips are available in variety stores at a small price. They protect hands, manicures, small cuts and scratches from water, detergents, smelly chopping jobs.

Grater: Sooner or later, you're going to have to grate something: potato, carrot, cheese, something. The standard kind of grater is a metal sheet or four-sided hollow metal column with holes punched from the inside, sharp metal projections on the outside on which the food is grated; the problem is that those projections are really sharp, and fingers can be shredded along with the food. Preferable for large items is the strong mesh type—strong enough to grate food, but not fingers. Best, in the author's view, is

the imported rotary grater that works for any food—
including all of those mentioned—that can be cut into
fairly small pieces: with this kind of grater, the food is put
into a small cuplike container, to be grated by the metal
projections on a cylinder rotated by turning a handle,
mechanically like the first type, except that your fingers
need never get near the grating surface. All graters should
be thoroughly cleaned after use, in order to prevent the
development of rust.

Many foods can also be grated in a blender.

Griddle: If you make pancakes, bacon, sausage, sunny-
side-up eggs with any frequency at all, this will be a good
thing to have. We mean, here, the kind that fits over one,
two, or more top-of-the-stove burners, as opposed to the
electric kind (see WAFFLE IRON). It lets you put together all the ingredients of, say, a Sunday brunch on one
utensil—usually made of super-gauge aluminum, easily
cleanable with steel-wool scouring pads.

Grill: If you do, or plan to do, a good deal of outdoor
cooking, your best investment is a portable on-wheels grill
that can be positioned as you like around your yard or
patio, according to wind direction or other factors. Look
for features like a wind shield, and a grid that's adjustable
as to height over the charcoal or coals that provide the
heat.

Ice Cube Trays: See REFRIGERATOR-FREEZER.

Jars: Save them—delabeled and thoroughly washed—for
such uses as storing leftovers; peanut butter and mayonnaise jars are especially useful sizes. Keep plastic ice
cream containers, too, for the same reasons.

Jar Opener: This simple clamp-and-turn device, sometimes called a jar wrench, is a lot better and faster than

tedious cap-tapping and holding under hot water; get one that accommodates both bottle caps and broad jar lids.

Kettle: You'll need a big one, at least 10- or 12-quart capacity, if you intend to cook big things like live lobsters and large quantities of soup.

Knife Sharpener: One may be attached to your electric can opener; if not, get a separate one—it's important for knives to be sharp.

Knives: Vital kitchen tools, these. Basic types are paring, carving, chopping, bread knives. It's vital, too, that you keep them sharp, or the carving knife won't carve, the chopping knife will bruise instead of chop. Sharpen knives frequently, and don't keep them in a drawer if you can help it; the kind of wooden wall rack that leaves the blades hanging free is best. Your knives will last longer, too, if you avoid immersing their handles in water.

Loaf Pans: You'll need them for baking anything loaf-shaped—bread, meat loaf, some kinds of cake—and for rectangular molds, mousses, aspics. Standard sizes are generally 4½ inches wide, about 2½ or 3 inches deep, from 8 to 12 inches long; it's good to own a couple of different sizes.

Masher, Potato: Obviously a necessity for mashed potatoes (unless you use the instant kind, which lack a certain something), a masher can be used, of course to mash other things too—hard-boiled eggs, for example, or cooked carrots.

Measuring Cups: No kitchen's complete, or even operative, without at least one set for dry measures, one set for liquids. See Chapter VII for a full rundown.

Measuring Spoons: You should own one or two sets of these. Again, see Chapter VII.

Melon-Ball Cutter: This tiny ice-cream-scoop gadget is very useful for cutting balls of cantaloupe, honeydew, and watermelon to combine in a cool summer dessert, but it's good for other things as well: making butter balls (well, they're fun to serve), making cream cheese balls to cover with crushed nuts for snacking, pulling things like olives and maraschino cherries out of jars.

Mitts, Oven: See POT HOLDERS.

Mixer: See EGGBEATER.

Muffin Tin: This specialized baking pan, generally available in 6- and 12-cup models, is useful not only for muffins, but for popovers and baked potatoes as well. Additionally, a muffin tin can be a good six-course infant serving dish.

Omelet Pan: A good thing to have if you intend to do omelets in the real French manner; it's a frying pan made of iron, about 2 inches deep, with an unusually long handle and a diameter of about 7 inches, available through import houses or restaurant suppliers. If you use the pan only for omelets, you don't ever wash it, but just wipe it clean with paper towels.

Oven: Clean it often, and don't let grease build up. Use an oven cleaner, and follow all directions very carefully. The oven door can be cleaned in between overall cleanings with baking soda on a damp cloth. Mainly, you're smart if you save on oven cleaning by lining the whole business with foil when something's likely to spatter, and by slipping a sheet of foil on the shelf below when something might possibly bubble over. (Also see BROILING PANS; ROTISSERIE; TOASTER.)

Paper-Towel Holder: Paper towels are now often sold in supersize rolls—which simply do not fit into the closed kind of dispenser, and may not fit into the open kind either, if it is mounted too close to the wall. If you want to be able to use that extra-fat kind of paper-towel roll, mount an open holder well away from the wall; measure first. If you already own, or prefer, the closed kind, then be sure to buy the standard-size roll.

Pastry Brush: It's called that, but it's really useful for a good many more things—anything, in fact, where you want to brush something (sauce, melted butter, whatever) on something (bread, poultry, meat, fish); a very basic culinary tool, we think.

Pie Plates: There are glass ones, metal ones, and disposable aluminum ones—all useful for more things than pies. They are good general baking dishes, for one thing. For another, they make good kinds of dishes on which to keep fresh meat in the refrigerator.

Piping Tube: This is the standard device for decorative frostings, and if you go in for that sort of thing, then buy one. If you don't, or if you do but only occasionally, you can probably make do, when the need arises, with a hunk of wax paper coiled in the form of an ice cream cone, a hole snipped at the tip.

Potato Peeler: A highly recommended gadget, this, that lets you peel potatoes, carrots, apples, whatever, quickly and cleanly, without the inadvertent waste that often occurs when one tries to remove the peel, and only the peel, with a knife.

Pot Holders: While one famous culinary artist, much seen on television, seems to find the nearest kitchen towel fine for grasping hot pots and pans, we personally think that a bit awkward; the author is specifically partial to the insulated mitt type that offers somewhat surer protection than the traditional small-square kind. Have at least two (you can't tote a roasting pan with one hand).

Pressure Cooker: This special top-of-the-stove device uses the scientific principle that temperature of a gas is proportional to pressure. It cooks by putting steam under very high pressure, up to double that of the surrounding atmosphere, so that its temperature is well above that of boiling water. Food such as vegetables can thus be cooked extra fast (see some representative times among the listings in Chapter VIII). Pressure cookers come in various sizes; the 3- or 4-quart size is most practical for the average family.

Range: Whether yours is a gas or electric type, just a reminder, here, that it should be wiped clean with a damp cloth after each use; cooked-on grease on burners can be removed by light use of a scouring pad. Don't forget the drip tray under the burners. And if your range has a hood with a filter, that filter should be taken out and cleaned frequently in sudsy water.

Refrigerator-Freezer: Easiest to care for, of course, is the kind that defrosts both parts automatically; some, though, have the automatic feature only for the refrigerator section, and in that case you must defrost the freezer, and should do so as soon as a ¼-inch layer of frost has built up. Put frozen foods in the refrigerator while you defrost the freezer, keep the refrigerator door closed, and the foods won't defrost during the hour or so that freezer defrosting will take. The refrigerator itself should be cleaned often, food spills wiped up immediately, and the entire interior washed every two or three weeks with a baking-soda solution. (These are, of course, generally suggestions; follow any specific directions that come with your particular appliance.) Two special notes on ice cube trays: put newly filled ones under trays of frozen cubes, and they'll freeze faster; don't use detergents, very hot water, or scouring pads on the trays—they'll take off the special wax finish that prevents cubes from sticking.

Ring Mold: Useful for any kind of molded desserts—gelatins, mousses—and aspics, a ring mold is a must if you go in for Austrian cookery, much inclined to such dishes.

Roasting Pan: You'll need at least one. Basic kinds are the lidless rectangular type, also usable for big baked dishes such as lasagne or chicken parts baked in a sauce, and the deep oval kind with a lid designed for large roasts of meat and poultry. The sturdiest roasting pans are made of heavy enameled metal with an ovenlike finish, or of stainless steel.

Roasting Rack: see CAKE RACKS.

Rolling Pin: It's the only way to prepare pie crust or cooky dough for baking. A rolling pin is also useful for crushing things like nuts or corn flakes (wrapped in wax paper first).

Rotisserie: This small electric oven roasts and broils, is useful for table-top cookery, and can provide an extra oven in situations where you must oven-cook two different things at the same time (as, for example, a cake to be baked and a chicken to be broiled). Some of the newest kitchens include a rotisserie as well as the standard oven and broiler as part of the built-in cooking equipment. For comment on another kind of extra oven, see TOASTER.

Saucepans: These are your basic cooking containers, and you should have several in various sizes from a cup or a cup and a half up to 3 or 4 quarts or more, all with well-fitting covers. They're available in a wide range of materials—stainless steel, copper, enameled metal, aluminum, combinations. For perfect French cookery, enameled or tin-lined copper saucepans are preferred, since steel or aluminum can discolor white sauces, and can also lend a slightly metallic taste to such vegetables as spinach; in other cooking, aluminum and steel are fine, and the combination of aluminum and stainless steel is excellent. There are also saucepans, like frying pans, available with Teflon coating.

Shears: You'll need them for cutting up poultry, small chunks of meat for stews, and so on. Get a really top-quality pair, and they'll last for years.

Sieves: Have several, for multiple straining and draining purposes; they should sit comfortably over a variety of bowls or saucepans. Our advice: start with a basic size such as a 6-inch diameter, add others in larger and smaller sizes as you see the need for them in your culinary routine.

Sink: Make a point of cleaning it after each dishwashing session; don't let stains sit. If you're scouring a large pot or pan, protect your sink's finish by resting the utensil on a folded dish cloth. Porcelain sinks should be cleaned with scouring powder (never a steel-wool soap pad), stainless steel sinks with dishwashing detergent.

Skewers: For barbecuing small cuts of meat and vegetables, and for Near Eastern dishes such as shish kebab, you'll need some of the long over-the-fire kind. For poultry-trussing and other holding-things-together uses, get a set of the small ones made for that purpose.

Spatulas: These lifters and turners of flat things such as pancakes are usually made of stainless steel, come in many sizes and styles—broad or narrow, long- or short-handled, plain or slotted, handles straight or set at an angle to the spatula surface. The author's own favorite happens to be a slotted one with a fairly short, angled handle—but which you'll use most will be a matter of your own preferences.

Whether or not you own any Teflon-coated frying pans —on which a metal spatula should normally never be used —the all-wood spatulas designed specifically for use with them will come in handy. The author finds one of these better than a spoon for stirring sauces in frying pans, for deglazing pans, for making scrambled eggs.

A wood-handled rubber spatula performs better than anything else for bowl-scraping and for cutting-and-folding operations.

Spoons: Your basic cooking spoons should include two types: one or more of the slotted or perforated kind for picking things out of cooking liquids; several wooden ones for stirring things while they're cooking, including a large, long one for stews, smaller ones for saucepan cookery. You may also want to have one or more large unslotted serving spoons for situations where you want cooking liquid or sauce to accompany the food.

Stove: See RANGE.

Teakettle: A closed kettle that whistles when the water boils offers two great advantages in the many situations in which a specific amount of boiling water is needed, ranging from tea- and coffee-making to dissolving of powder for fruit gelatin. First, the water boils faster in the closed container, and since it tells you when it's ready, needn't be hovered over. Secondly, since none boils away, you measure the water when you pour it into the kettle, and you know the amount will be precisely right.

Thermometers: You should own three, perhaps four: one for the refrigerator, one for the oven, one meat thermometer—plus one for candy-making if that's something you do. See Chapters V and VIII for full discussions of food-keeping and cooking temperatures.

Timer: Your range or oven, if you're lucky, may have a timer built in; if not, buy one, making sure it's accurate down to one minute and that it's equipped with a clearly audible time's-up bell. Some of the best ones are available, at small cost, in photo-supply stores.

Toaster: You can get the standard pop-up type, of course, accommodating two, four, or more slices, but the author is partial to the glass-doored kind that performs multiple functions—toasts (and lets you watch the progress of the toasting), browns, also functions as an extra oven for keeping things warm, heating heat-and-serve foods, baking small items such as potatoes and small meat loaves.

Tongs: Tongs, in the author's opinion, work better than a fork or other utensil for many purposes; among them: turning bacon, turning meat slices or chicken pieces being fried or broiled, fishing corn on the cob out of boiling water.

Waffle Iron: A waffle iron isn't really a basic necessity, not even a practical buy if you don't like or make waffles, since its other functions can be filled by other things; if you do have one essentially for waffle-making, though, it's handy to know that it can—with a change or reversal of cooking surfaces—make eggs or pancakes too, can even double as a hot plate with the addition of a sheet of foil.

Whisks: For one-hand beating, wire whisks are excellent; they range in size from quite small to gigantic, and are good for everything from mixing pancake batter to blending sauces to beating eggs—and a proper French chef wouldn't beat eggs any other way.

XII. And a Nice Little Wine

Huge volumes have been written on the subject of wines—selecting them, serving them, cooking with them. Since this is not a book but a mere chapter, we'll try to be as concise as possible. Mostly, we'll be concerned with the subject of serving, and chiefly the what-goes-with-what question.

First, though, a brief comment on the use of wine in cooking. So far as main dishes go, wine's used mostly in marinades and in long-cooking things such as stews and braised things, sauces and soups; that's because you want the alcohol to cook away, leaving the flavor behind. You'll find wine used more in recipes for French or Italian dishes than in others.

If sherry is called for in a sauce or gravy recipe, a fairly dry kind is meant, a "cooking sherry" or the kind used as an appetizer or aperitif wine (we'll come to the various categories shortly). Red table wine? Choose a light Burgundy or a Bordeaux or keep a bottle of inexpensive dry red wine on hand for cooking purposes. When white wine's called for, any good dry one will do, including dry vermouth. Of course, if the recipe calls for a specific kind—as in Veal Marsala—it's important to choose that type for authentic results.

In dessert dishes wine is also sometimes used—notably in puddings and sauces, or poured over sugared fruit such as berries or melon balls. The ones used most often are Madeira, port, or one of the sweeter white table wines such as Sauterne.

Few of us have wine cellars these days. As a practical rule, simply keep your wine in the coolest, driest part of your home. If it's corked, it should be kept on its side and rotated once in a while, in order to keep the cork moist (trying to remove a dry, crumbling cork can be a downright traumatic experience); wine racks for this purpose are widely available and can be as plain or fancy as you like. For opening such bottles, the kind of corkscrew with two handles works best. Wine with a screw cap can be kept standing up.

One general comment before we get into the facts of wine serving. Don't be intimidated by the wine snobbery that prevails in some quarters. It's true that you can spend a great deal for wine; but it's also true that some fine-tasting wines, both imported and domestic, are quite inexpensive. Further, though many French and other imported wines are excellent, so are many American-made wines; some of the world's nicest wines are produced in California and New York. And though we're going to talk about what kinds of wine go best with various kinds of food, and the suggestions will generally make for the most pleasant eating and drinking, they are just that—suggestions, to be followed or flouted according to your own likes and dislikes.

MAIN TYPES OF WINE

There are a number of ways to classify wines, some based on fairly esoteric facets of the wine-making process. Our breakdown here is among the generally accepted ones, and the one we think least confusing.

Appetizer Wines, often flavored or fortified, are meant to be served before the meal, generally accompanying canapés, dips, hors d'oeuvres, cheeses, and such. How they are served and what they're served in depends on personal preference.

This group includes the vermouths, both dry (white) and sweet (red); the in-between to dry sherries such as Amontillado, Fino, Amoroso, and Oloroso; and a number of special-formula brand-name wines (some of the latter are U.S. brands, but the most popular are French, and usually carry the phrase "an aperitif wine" beneath the brand name). All of these can be served straight, chilled or not, with or without ice, as you like; some—most familiarly, vermouth—combine with liquors to make cocktails, as well as with other things like club soda.

Red Table Wines, or Dinner Wines, are those served with a main course that usually includes red meat, though some are appropriate with poultry as well, and the Italian reds traditionally accompany pasta. They are rich, full-bodied, and dry. Red table wines should ideally be served at what is loosely referred to as "room temperature," but means something between 65° and 70°. Open the wine about an hour before serving to let it "breathe." It is best served in a basic tulip-shaped glass of 6- to 10-ounce capacity; the glass should be only about half filled, though, to allow the drinker to enjoy the pleasant aroma or "bouquet" of the wine.

There are three general classifications of French red table wines, some of which have lent their names to similar wines produced elsewhere. They are the Red Burgundies such as Chambertin and Côte de Nuits and the somewhat lighter Beaujolais and Pommard; Red Bordeaux (in the U.S. referred to as clarets) such as Pomerol and St. Émilion and the lighter Graves and Médoc; rich Rhône wines, the best known of which is Châteauneuf-du-Pape.

Italian reds include Chianti and Bardolino—the former

resembling the French Burgundy, the latter a bit lighter, more like Bordeaux. In the U.S., the Napa and Sonoma wines from California are prominent red types, as are our domestic Burgundies and Zinfandels (the latter are similar to Bordeaux) and our Red Pinot and Pinot Noir, which have a Burgundy-like quality. The Spanish wine-makers also produce excellent, very dry Burgundies.

White Table Wines, or Dinner Wines, are primarily served with light-colored main-course dishes—chicken, fish and shellfish, egg dishes; most are dry, but some are sweet or semisweet. They should be served chilled (two to three hours in the refrigerator), in the same sort of glass as the red table wines.

Among the best-known French white wines are the light, dry ones such as Chablis, Muscadet, Pouilly-Fuissé, and Pouilly-Fumé; the fuller-bodied White Burgundies, such as Meursault and Montrachet, the White Rhône wines, and White Bordeaux like Graves; the semisweet Anjou; the distinctly sweeter Sauternes; the Barsac, falling somewhere between the last two types in sweetness.

A number of other countries, including our own, also produce excellent white wines. German and Alsatian white are deservedly famed; among the best are Moselle, Niersteiner, the Rhine wines, the very light Riesling, Sylvaner, Traminer. Gumpoldskirchner is a particularly good Austrian white wine. There is a Chilean Riesling. From Italy come a White Chianti, dry to semisweet Orvieto, and dry Soave. Many of the European terms are used by U.S. producers as well, and usually correspond in character, though our Sauternes are not always as definitely sweet as the French; our white Alameda and Napa wines are also distinctive.

Rosé Wines are also table wines, neither red nor white, but pink; they go particularly well with ham or pork, but have the happy faculty of combining well with other main dishes as well. They should be served in the same way as white table wines.

Most rosé wines—such as the French Provence and Tavel—are definitely dry; their Anjou, however, is slightly sweet. Italian rosés are dry, while the rosés of Portugal, which enjoy a reputation for high quality, may vary. Our domestic rosé wines are on the dry, light side; Gamay, Grenache, and Grignolino are the best-known varieties.

Dessert Wines are, as their name implies, served with dessert; they are usually not served with extremely sweet desserts, but rather with fruits, cheeses, cookies, or rather light and simple cakes. They should be served at room temperature, in the same sort of glass as a dinner wine (though the glass is not so important with a dessert wine).

Chief among the dessert wines are the Cream Sherries, which originated in Spain but are now produced in many countries; another major dessert wine, Malaga, is also of Spanish origin. Portugal contributed the ports—ruby port, and the slightly drier tawny port—as well as Madeira. Marsala is of Italian origin, Muscatel from France.

Sparkling Wines may be served at any time, with anything at all, but are not very generally used as table wines; they are rather reserved for special occasions or, if on the sweet side, served with desserts. They must be served chilled (for at least four hours), and once chilled must be kept chilled; unlike other wines, once they have been opened, any remainder must be discarded. They are usually served in the broad, shallow, traditional champagne glass—but it's up to you.

The best known types are Champagne, Sparkling Burgundy and the Italian Asti Spumante. The Burgundies are fairly dry, the Spumante generally sweet. Champagne may run the full range from dry to sweet, and the terms used for it—in that order—are Brut (driest); Extra Sec, or Extra Dry; Sec, or Dry: Demi-Sec, or Demi-Dry; Doux or Sweet (sweetest).

WHAT TO SERVE

Appetizer and dessert wines have been fairly well delineated in the preceding section, and sparkling wines, as noted, are servable any time, with anything. The listing that follows concerns table wines for main courses—the main problem. If in doubt, you can often rely on the knowledgeable gentlemen who own and manage our wine and liquor stores, especially in metropolitan areas; they are usually delighted to give advice, can often gear suggestions to your budget limitations, too. Also, the way you cook any particular dishes in which you specialize may have a certain influence; if you find that a particular wine goes well with a dish in which you excel and in which your friends delight—by all means stick to it, though you might from time to time try others in the same family.

Beef: Any of the fuller-bodied red Burgundy or Bordeaux wines—of the nature of Chambertin, St. Émilion, Zinfandel—or Rhônes will be best, but any red wine you like is fine.

Cheese Dishes: Choose from any of the white wines, from dry to sweet, according to your own tastes; or serve a rosé.

Chicken: Any white wine goes with chicken, as does rosé; the light red Bordeaux, such as Médoc, are also right, particularly with roast chicken. With fricassee, a somewhat heavier wine—a full-bodied White Burgundy, or a White Rhône or White Graves—will often be best.

Duck: Usually duck tastes best with a red wine—a Burgundy, Rhône, or Bordeaux, according to your own tastes. If you're serving it with a fruit sauce (*Canard à l'Orange*, for example), a full-bodied White Burgundy may be interesting.

Egg Dishes: Best bets are any of the light white wines, or perhaps a rosé.

Fish: Any of the white wines, ranging from the semi-sweet Anjous to the snappy, lusty German ones, will go well with fish; the fuller-bodied whites such as Meursault and the White Rhônes are especially good if there is a sauce involved; a rosé mates well with fish, too.

Goose: This a red-wine bird, like duck; Beaujolais, Pommard, or Châteauneuf-du-Pape are usually the happiest choices.

Ham: The wine of choice is one of the lighter reds, such as a Graves or Médoc—or a rosé.

Lamb: Basically, the lighter red Burgundies work best, a Beaujolais or a Pommard, but the fuller-bodied Bordeaux are fine, too. With a lamb stew or braised dish, the fuller-bodied white wines, such as the Burgundies or Rhônes, are also good.

Liver: Red-to-pink table wines are right with liver: the lighter red Burgundies or Beaujolais, or a dry rosé.

Lobster: Full-bodied white wines such as Burgundies or Graves are excellent. (Also see SHELLFISH.)

Mussels: Mussels take especially well to the lightest,

most piquant white wines—Muscadet, Pouilly-Fuissé, and Pouilly-Fumé. (Also see SHELLFISH.)

Pasta: Spaghetti and macaroni dishes, whatever their sauces, go well with the Italian red wines or with any of the Burgundy types.

Pork: Rosé is the wine of choice with pork, though a White Rhône or other full-bodied white will work nicely. If pork chops are braised in a dark sauce, a light red wine can also be a good selection.

Poultry: Generally speaking, white wines are equal choices with the lighter reds. (Also see listings of individual types of poultry.)

Shellfish: Top choice is a very dry, light white wine such as Muscadet (a super-dry type), Chablis, or Pouilly; a White Burgundy is also good. The important point is that the wine be dry and white. (Also see LOBSTER; MUSSELS.)

Sweetbreads: Choice of wine depends, here, upon how they're cooked. If the sauce is a white one, then a light, dry white such as Chablis, or a Rhine wine, will be best; if they're served in a brown sauce, then choose a rosé or a light red wine such as a Graves or Médoc.

Veal: The light red Bordeaux are the usually safe choices, though there are exceptions: if a light sauce is involved, a White Burgundy or Bordeaux can be interesting accompaniment; if the veal is stewed, a rosé would be equally nice.

XIII.   Something of Value

Food is a source of enjoyment, of course, and of creative satisfaction for the cook as well. But it's a source of many more things, too—things we literally can't live without. In this chapter, we record some of those.

You need to eat to stay alive—as almost everyone knows. You also need to derive specific nutrients from your food; mere eating won't necessarily give you those, unless you've planned to include them. They include vitamins, minerals, and other factors—over forty essentials, all told; we list just the main ones here, since if you make a point of including those in your menu, you're reasonably sure of getting the others as well.

VITAMINS

There are about twenty of these, though only some six to eight are of major concern; they govern a good deal of your growth and functioning. All that your body normally requires will be provided if you eat a well-balanced diet that includes a good selection of vitamin-rich foods. Under certain conditions—such as pregnancy, or a specifically diagnosed deficiency—your physician may prescribe supplementary vitamins, either singly or in multiple form. Except under such circumstances, the taking of vitamin supplements is neither necessary nor desirable; it is possible to get too much for one's own good of certain vitamins, and ingesting unneeded amounts of the others is simply a waste of money.

There are four major vitamins or vitamin groups:

Vitamin A: An essential growth factor for youngsters, Vitamin A plays a part in maintaining good vision at all ages, as well as the health of the skin and mucous membranes. Liver, eggs, butter, milk and cream, cheese, and fish-liver oils are excellent sources, as are green and yellow vegetables (notably spinach, greens, carrots, yellow squash, and sweet potatoes); the vegetables contain substances called carotenes, which are readily converted by the body itself to Vitamin A. While ordinary margarine is not a source, most margarine is now fortified with Vitamin A or with carotene. There is also a limited amount of Vitamin A in a few other fruits and vegetables, among them apricots, cantaloupe, and tomatoes.

The B Vitamins: Not a single vitamin but a group or "complex," the B vitamins include thiamine (also known as Vitamin B_1), riboflavin (also sometimes called Vitamin B_2 and sometimes Vitamin G), niacin, folic acid, and Vitamin B_{12}; there are others, but these five are the ones that medical science knows most about thus far. Folic acid and Vitamin B_{12} are somehow important to the health of the blood. Thiamine, riboflavin, and niacin are essential for conversion of fuel into energy, and for general maintenance of steady nerves, healthy skin, normal appetite, good digestion, and emotional well-being; thiamine operates in nervous tissues, riboflavin in the cells' oxidation processes, niacin in the utilization of sugars.

Extreme deficiencies in this group can cause serious disease—beriberi in the case of a lack of thiamine, pellagra when niacin is missing, extensive scaling and a breakdown in the digestive processes when there is a riboflavin deficiency. Such severe symptoms are rarely seen now, but results of mild deficiencies—nervousness, listlessness, a vague lack of a feeling of well-being—are more common.

By far the best sources of B vitamins: whole-grain or enriched bread, flour, and cereals. Milk and milk products such as cheeses are also good sources, especially of riboflavin. And a significant amount of B-complex vitamins are also derived from meats, fish, greens, cabbage, lettuce, beans, nuts, and eggs.

Vitamin C: Also called ascorbic acid, Vitamin C helps to keep all the body's tissues in good condition, playing a major role in circulation and in promoting good teeth and healthy gums, and in keeping up strength and the ability to resist infection. Vitamin C cannot be stored by the body at all, so it is imperative that it be a part of the daily diet. A serious deficiency will cause scurvy, a disease that afflicted many seafarers on ocean voyages of many months' duration, until it was discovered that the simple inclusion of citrus fruits among the ship's stores would prevent the problem; milder Vitamin C deficiency may be evidenced by tender and/or bleeding gums, painful joints, or weakened muscles.

Citrus fruits—oranges, lemons, tangerines, limes, grapefruit—are the prime source of Vitamin C, and tomatoes, strawberries, and cantaloupe are also good providers. Cabbage contains a fairly substantial amount of this vitamin, as do such green vegetables as broccoli, brussels sprouts, green peppers, kale, and spinach; cauliflower, potatoes, and sweet potatoes also offer moderate amounts. In paring fruits and vegetables, incidentally, pare as thinly as possible; the greatest concentration of vitamin content tends to be close to the skin.

Vitamin D: The "sunshine vitamin" is essential for the body's assimilation of calcium and some other minerals; it is especially vital for the young (a severe deficiency can cause rickets and other malformations of the bones and teeth) and for pregnant women and nursing mothers, though people of both sexes and all ages have a continuing need for it.

Summer sunlight is indeed a top "source" of Vitamin D, though the terminology's not quite accurate; what happens is that certain substances in the skin are changed, under the influence of direct sunlight, into the vitamin. Significant food sources are egg yolks, butter, codfish, clams and oysters, salmon, tuna, sardines, fortified milk, and fortified margarine.

MINERALS

Minerals, like vitamins, are essential to certain basic bodily functioning; they work alone, in combination with one another, or—as already mentioned—hand-in-glove with vitamins. Among the major ones:

Calcium: Calcium, like Vitamin D, is most crucial for growing youngsters, though it's needed by older folks as well. It's stored by the body, about 99 percent of it used for bones and teeth; a tiny but vital percent circulates in the blood, and is essential to proper working of muscles and nerves. A calcium deficiency will generally affect the bones—in children with possible malformation, in older people with brittleness and bones that are easily broken.

Top sources of calcium are milk (whole or skim) and milk products such as buttermilk and cheeses. Greens, especially turnip greens and mustard greens, offer substantial amounts of this mineral. A few other vegetables— notably broccoli, celery, cabbage, cauliflower, chard, carrots, onions, green beans, and asparagus—also contain some calcium, as do whole-grain foods and egg yolks.

Iron: Iron is essential for good circulation, and a severe deficiency can cause anemia; the need for iron can vary with age, sex, and other individual factors. Liver is the iron source par excellence, but dark green vegetables such as spinach also contain a good deal of it. Other iron-containing menu items include egg yolks, meats and poultry, dried fruits, molasses, whole-grain breads and cereals, clams and oysters, and a few additional vegetables —peas and beans, cauliflower, celery, chard, lettuce— also contain a small amount.

Iodine: You need a small but vital amount of iodine to keep your thyroid gland working properly; a deficiency of this mineral results in hypothyroidism and a marked swelling of the gland (goiter). The iodine source is sea water, and if you live along a coast, you needn't give the question another thought; you're getting some iodine in your drinking water, as well as in locally grown foods. Inland, however, you should make a point of using iodized salt; if you do so regularly, that will be sufficient protection— though you might want to put salt-water fish or shellfish on your menu about three or four times a month, just for a little extra insurance.

Other Minerals: You also need small amounts of a few other minerals, though you need give no special thought to them; if you eat a generally balanced diet, they'll be there, and they usually work along with other food elements. Among them are copper (which works with iron), phosphorus (which works in conjunction with calcium and Vitamin D), magnesium, and sodium.

OTHER ESSENTIALS

Three other elements, in addition to vitamins and minerals, are important for good nutrition and should be included in a wisely planned diet.

Protein is the chief substance of which the body—muscles, organs, and other tissues—is composed; it is vital in building those tissues, and also in repairing and renewing them. New protein must be added daily; the body isn't capable of storing much of it, and it's constantly needed to combat normal wear and tear. Protein deficiency, one of the most tragic sorts of malnutrition, is little seen now in our country, but is still all too common in some parts of the world, particularly in certain tropical areas. Chronic deficiency in adults, while serious—edema and liver disorders are two symptoms—is not so severe as the impact on growing youngsters; in small children, severe protein deficiency causes a disease called kwashiorkor, with digestive malfunction, rashes, swelling, permanent mental and physical retardation, and eventually—if the deficiency continues untreated—death.

Animals, like human beings, are composed chiefly of protein; thus, foods from animal sources are our best source of protein: meats, poultry, fish, eggs, milk, milk products such as cheese. Vegetable sources are second best, but in the absence of animal proteins, soybeans, nuts, dry beans, and peas do offer significant quantities. A third group of foods—whole-grain cereals and breads, fruits, vegetables in general—have some protein content, but the relatively inferior protein in these foods is far more powerful, nutritionally, when eaten not alone, but in combination with foods from the first group. Thus, the vegetables will actually be more nutritious if eaten with meat, a youngster's cereal more helpful if eaten with milk than if nibbled as a snack.

Fats: In addition to functioning as a heat and energy source, fats supply certain fatty acids that act to guard the skin against some eczemas and dermatoses; some also contain Vitamins A and D, or assist the body in making use of these vitamins. It's usually not necessary to make an extra effort to include fats in one's diet, since many foods—meats, egg yolks, whole milk and milk products, for example—include fats; butter on bread is a fat source; vegetable fats count, too, so that fats are derived from fried foods, salad dressings, and the like. The body does store fat, so doesn't need a new supply daily.

Carbohydrates: These are the starches and sugars, functioning chiefly as suppliers of heat and energy; they are stored in the body for use as needed—especially the starches, which the body first converts to fats and storable forms of sugar. Fruits are excellent sources of natural sugar.

PLOTTING AND PLANNING

All this valuable information should, of course, be translated into wise buying and menu planning for your family's nutritional benefit. To aid in that effort, the U.S. Department of Agriculture has plotted a per-week rundown based on standards set by the National Research Council. Based on age and sex, the USDA recommends *weekly* consumptions of various types of food by moderately active people; see table, page 203. If you're more or less active than most, the amounts should be adjusted: you'll need to eat a bit more if you're a football player; if you're fairly sedentary and overweight, you should eat less of the fats and carbohydrates that offer relatively little nutritional value compared with meats, fruits, and vegetables.

When the chart shows a range of quantities for children, the smaller is for younger children; for men and women, a range means smaller quantities for those over fifty-five, who are usually less active; in the last column, it is the nursing mother who needs to eat more. The meat amounts shown for children from one to six, girls thirteen to nineteen, and pregnant and nursing women should include some liver, for extra iron.

USDA Recommended Amounts per Week

	Children 1 - 6	Children 7 - 12	Girls 13 - 19	Boys 13 - 19	Men	Women	Pregnant & Nursing Women
Milk & milk products	6 qts.	6-6½ qts.	7 qts.	7 qts.	3½ qts.	3½ qts.	7-10 qts.
Meat, poultry, & fish	1½-2 lbs.	3-4 lbs.	4½ lbs.	5-5½ lbs.	5-5½ lbs.	4-4½ lbs.	4-5 lbs.
Eggs	6	7	7	7	7	6	7
Dry beans & peas, nuts	1 oz.	2-4 oz.	2 oz.	4-6 oz.	2-4 oz.	2 oz.	2 oz.
Whole-grain or enriched breads, cereals, etc.	1-1½ lbs.	2-3 lbs.	2½-3 lbs.*	4-5 lbs.	3-4 lbs.	2-2½ lbs.	2-3 lbs.
Citrus fruits & tomatoes	1½-2 lbs.	2½ lbs.	2½ lbs.	3 lbs.	2½-3 lbs.	2½ lbs.	3½-5 lbs.
Dk. green & deep yellow vegetables	¼ lb.	½-¾ lb.	¾ lb.	¾ lb.	¾ lb.	¾ lb.	1½ lbs.
Potatoes	½-1 lb.	1½-2½ lbs.	2 lbs.	3-4 lbs.	2-3 lbs.	1-1½ lbs.	1½-3 lbs.
Other vegetables & fruits	3½ lbs.	5½ lbs.	6 lbs.	7 lbs.	5-7 lbs.	4-6 lbs.	6-6½ lbs.
Fats & oils	¼-⅓ lb.	½-¾ lb.	¾ lb.	1-1¼ lbs.	¾-1 lb.	½ lb.	½-¾ lb.
Sweets & sugars	¼-⅔ lb.	¾ lb.	¾ lb.	1-1¼ lbs.	1-1½ lbs.	½-1 lb.	¾ lb.

*Larger quantity is in this case for younger girls.

XIV. The Calorie Question and Other Special Problems

The nutritional facts and figures spelled out in Chapter XIII prevail for most people, under most conditions. But if you're substantially overweight, or there's some special condition that can be affected, one way or another, by what you eat—then you're not most people. In this chapter, a postscript to the last one: some guidelines on those special situations.

THE CALORIE QUESTION

A calorie, in you or in a chemistry lab, is a unit of heat and energy. Aside from its other functions, all food is fuel; it gives you the energy to keep yourself and your activities going. All food thus has calories—though some foods have a good deal more, or a good deal fewer, than others. Some foods, as we've already noted, have in fact little else to offer; when you eat such foods, if your body simply has no use for the energy (or already has reserves on which to draw), it is stored—mostly in the form of fat. It follows, then, that if you consume fewer calories your body will then turn to its energy storehouse to fill its needs—and you will lose weight.

Even under ordinary circumstances, calorie needs can vary, for a fairly active person, with weight, sex, and age. An average 120-pound girl of eighteen or twenty, for example, may need about 2000 calories a day to maintain her weight—while her forty-five-year-old mother whose proper weight is 130 will only need about 1900, since she is less active and no longer growing. Similarly, a twenty-five-year-old man whose best weight is 165 needs about 3100 calories a day—while his fifty-five-year-old father of exactly the same weight needs only about 2600. If your weight stays about right, you're getting the right amount of calories for you; if you're overweight, you're getting too many. (And overweight is, incidentally, a health hazard at any age, an especially serious one if you're over thirty-five—when it can help foster circulatory and kidney problems and ailments.)

Calorie-count listings will not be included here; there are a number of publications available that list them fully and accurately. Though we don't advocate your sitting down to each meal with pencil and paper, owning a calorie counter can help you to get familiar with some of the relative counts; the trick, you see, is to modify what you eat, and if you're aware of the rules, it's really not necessary to get involved in constant counting.

First, try to eliminate high-calorie extras: gravy on meats, butter on vegetables, cream in coffee, sugar on fruit, after-dinner candies, and the like. And remember, too, such hidden calories as the ones in fat used for frying (just about anything that can be fried can also be broiled or baked).

Then, within food categories, switch from high-calorie ones to those with fewer calories (remembering to keep amounts the same, though—double helpings of certain low-calorie foods can give you just as many calories as single helpings of foods high in calories); ounce for ounce, you can eat the same amount, but acquire fewer calories (and pounds). Some examples:

MEATS—Avoid pork, lamb, roasts; turn to calves' liver, steak.

POULTRY—Eat chicken, not goose.

FISH—Choose haddock, sole, cod, or flounder instead of perch or mackerel.

VEGETABLES—Fill your plate with greens, tomatoes, asparagus, mushrooms, snap beans, cauliflower, spinach—instead of potatoes, lima beans, corn, or peas.

SOUPS—Shun cream soups and chowders, fill up on vegetable soup, broths.

BEVERAGES—Drink skim milk or buttermilk instead of whole milk; coffee or tea instead of cocoa; citrus and tomato juices rather than fancy fruit "nectars"; low-calorie sodas instead of the regular kind. (Note: as this book goes to press, the U.S. Food and Drug Administration has warned that consuming large quantities of the substances used to artificially sweeten the low-calorie soft drinks may be unsafe. Until their safety is definitely established, it is recommended that consumption be limited to 4 or 5 12- or 16-ounce bottles per day to adults, 1½ bottles for children.)

It's perfectly possible—easy, in fact—to fill all your basic nutritional needs while still holding calories to a minimum. Get your *Vitamin A* from carrots, liver, kale, eggs, fortified skim milk, broccoli, greens; your *B Vitamins* from lean meat, skim milk, greens, a little enriched bread (buy it unsliced, slice it extra-thin to cut calories per slice); your *Vitamin C* from citrus fruits (most sources of this vitamin are low-calorie); your *Vitamin D* from eggs, fortified skim milk, codfish, leafy vegetables; your **protein** from lean beef, chicken, fish, skim milk, eggs; your **calcium** from skim milk, buttermilk, greens; your **iron** from liver, lean beef, chicken, eggs, clams and oysters, spinach. All these foods are relatively low-calorie ones, and very nutritious.

OTHER SPECIAL PROBLEMS

Most other problems of a physical nature need, and should get, medical advice. No radical subtractions from, or additions to, a balanced diet should be made without your doctor's say-so, and the comments that follow are very general ones—to be applied individually only if your own physician thinks it wise.

Acne: All doctors agree that so far as food goes, a good, balanced diet is essential during the teen years. Many feel, too, that it's smart to completely avoid certain foods; the ones most commonly cited as contributors to the problem are nuts, shellfish, pork, alcohol, colas and other sweet drinks, spices, fried foods, all extra fats and oils, all rich desserts, chocolate, sharp cheeses.

Allergy: The allergy victim must avoid the offending food or other substance; that's the only effective protection. What to avoid depends, of course, on the particular allergy, but in general, among the things that are common villains in food allergies are chocolate, various fish and shellfish, nuts, pork, tomatoes, alcohol, strawberries, various spices; it usually takes an expert to isolate the single culprit.

Cholesterol: If your doctor has advised you to avoid foods containing cholesterol, he's referring to foods containing animal fats: fat meats, oily fish (particularly oily ones are salmon, sardines, tuna), fatty poultry such as duck, whole milk and whole-milk products (cheeses, ice cream, cream, butter), lard or bacon fat used in frying, too many eggs (since eggs contain a number of important nutrients, they will usually not be cut out entirely; the patient on a low-cholesterol diet will often be advised to eat only a limited number, perhaps three or four a week).

Diabetes: If you or someone in your family has diabetes, don't make the mistake of leaping to dietary conclusions based on your past knowledge of someone else who may have been similarly afflicted. Diabetes is a metabolic disorder, which means that symptoms, reactions, and controls will differ from one individual to another. Your own doctor's judgment must prevail; whether he tells you not to worry about what you eat, or gives you very strict instructions—follow his advice faithfully.

Pregnancy: A basic balanced diet (see the preceding chapter) is the starting point for the mother-to-be; it's important that good health be maintained, for both mother's and baby's sake. Since the growing baby derives his nutritional benefits from his mother's diet, and his job is essentially a matter of building bones and other tissues, the obstetrician may suggest certain diet additions—extra calcium, iron, protein, possibly supplementary Vitamin D. He may also suggest cutting down on things clearly not essential for baby's growth, such as sugars and starches, to prevent inordinate weight gain on the mother's part; a gain of approximately 18 to 20 pounds—about 14 of those accounted for by the baby himself, the placenta and surrounding fluids, etc.—is usual. The obstetrician will also be concerned about the general health of the mother-to-be; the growing baby will automatically take whatever nutrients he needs—thus, if the supply is inadequate, leaving the mother with a dietary deficiency; leg cramps, for instance, are a common sign that there's not quite enough calcium to go around. Whatever advice your own doctor offers should be followed.

XV. Food Stains and Spills

Your kitchen sink, floor, work table, and—if you're smart—the walls around your work area as well, are of course meant to take splashes and spills, and the only note we need add here is: wipe fast, as soon as the splash or spill occurs, and before the food in question cakes, hardens, or whatever it will do if it's left to sit or cling long enough.

This chapter is concerned chiefly with foodstuffs that find their way onto your clothing, or that of your family. There are some tried-and-true, at least *usually* true, ways to cope with certain substances, which will be listed alphabetically. But first, a few general rules to follow:

(1) Get stains out—or have someone get them out—as soon as possible; by and large, the longer a stain remains, the harder it is to remove.

(2) If you don't know whether or not something is washable, assume it's not. (Of course this is one of the reasons it's a good idea to save hang tags, with the identity of the garments marked on them.)

(3) When you're dealing with clothing you know is washable, and you don't find the kind of stain listed herein (or you're not sure what the food was), and it's a fairly fresh spot—you're pretty safe starting by sponging with cold water. Put a paper towel underneath to absorb the stain as it comes out of the fabric.

(4) When using spot removers or cleaning fluids, be sure to follow the directions and precautions exactly as they pertain to kinds of stains, fabrics, procedures, and surrounding conditions. Usually, these include letting the spot dry before using the product. Unless the label specifically advises it, don't use such products on leather, rubber, plastic, rayon, or acetate.

(5) Some spot-removal methods can ruin certain fabrics, especially nonwashable ones. Before attacking the spot, try the method or product out first on some hidden or inside area.

(6) Trust your dry-cleaning man. The procedures that follow are all make-do emergency ones, so far as dry-cleanable clothes are concerned; the professional is always your best bet. And always tell him, too (if you yourself know), the exact nature of spots or stains; he can then give them informed special treatment and attention.

Here, then, are the wisest ways to cope with some of the more common food stains and spills.

Blood from Meat: If the garment is washable, soak it in cold water until the stain has paled considerably; then wash it in warm (not hot) water. Nonwashable things should be gently sponged with lukewarm water, then let dry, before dry-cleaning.

Cheese: Scrape off as much as possible, and sponge with cold water. Then wash as usual, or have dry-cleaned.

Chocolate: To get out chocolate or cocoa stains on washables, wash as usual; if any stain remains, treat with a weak bleaching solution, then wash again. For a nonwashable garment, scrape off what you can, sponge with warm water, and let it dry completely; then treat with cleaning fluid or spot remover, or have the garment dry-cleaned.

Coffee: A fresh coffee spot on a washable item should be attacked with boiling water, poured through the fabric with as much force as possible; stretch the garment, wrong side up, across the sink or over a large bowl, and pour the boiling water through from as high up as you can get. If the stain's not a fresh one, try a mild bleach. A fresh coffee stain on a nonwashable garment should be sponged with warm water; this will at least dissolve any sugar. If it's an old stain (or when the fresh stain is completely dry), use cleaning fluid or have the garment dry-cleaned.

Cream: see MILK.

Egg: Start, if the stain's fresh, by scraping off as much as you can. If the garment's washable, wash it as usual, soaking it in cold water for a while first; if it's not washable, sponge the spot with cool water, let it dry, then try some cleaning fluid. An old egg stain on washable clothing should be softened by rubbing in a little glycerine, then soaked in warm water, before washing.

Fruit: If the fruit in question is cherry, peach, pear, or plum, start by sponging with cold water, then rub in a little glycerine and let that sit for a few hours; following that, sponge with a few drops of vinegar, wait two minutes, and wash as usual, if the garment's washable (if not, sponge quickly with cool water, and let dry before dry-cleaning). Other fruits: handle the same way as COFFEE.

Gravy: Soak washables in cool water, then wash as usual. Nonwashables will need spot remover, cleaning fluid, or dry-cleaning.

Grease or Oil: Wet the spot, if the garment's washable; rub in some soap and as much baking powder as you can, and let sit for half an hour; then wash as usual, in hot water. Let grease stain on a nonwashable fabric dry, then treat with cleaning fluid or have dry-cleaned.

Ice Cream: Sponge the spot with lukewarm water, let it dry, and then wash or dry-clean. If a chocolate or fruit stain still remains, see those listings for how to cope.

Jam: Wash as usual (presoaking in lukewarm water will be an extra help), or dry-clean. (Also see FRUIT.)

Ketchup: Handle the same way as cherry, etc., stains (see FRUIT).

Liquor: Sponge quickly with cool water to dilute the liquor, then wash or dry-clean as usual.

Milk or Cream: For washable garments, simply wash as usual. Nonwashables should be sponged with lukewarm water, let dry completely; then treat with cleaning fluid or have dry-cleaned.

Mustard: Sponge the spot with cool water, rub in a little glycerine, then sponge with warm water and wash; if the garment is nonwashable, let the spot dry completely after the warm-water sponging, then treat with cleaning fluid or have dry-cleaned.

Tea: Handle the same way as COFFEE.

Wine: If the garment is washable, simply wash it. If it is not, and the wine is red, let the stain dry; if the wine's white, sponge with lukewarm water, then let dry. When the garment is dry, treat with cleaning fluid or have dry-cleaned.

Current SIGNET Movie and Television Tie-In Titles

☐ **2001: A SPACE ODYSSEY, a novel by Arthur C. Clarke based on the screenplay by Stanley Kibrick and Arthur C. Clarke.** A brilliant projection into the future, tracing man's lonely search among the stars for his intelligent equal, or master. Based on the MGM motion picture starring Keir Dullea and Gary Lockwood.
(#Q3580—95¢)

☐ **KRAKATOA, EAST OF JAVA by Michael Avallone.** The world's greatest volcano provides a terrifying obstacle for the shipmates who dared to venture into uncharted seas. Soon to be a major motion picture starring Maximilian Schell. (#P3797—60¢)

☐ **ROWAN AND MARTIN'S LAUGH-IN #1 compiled from material written by the Laugh-In writers.** It's chicken jokes, party time, graffiti, etc. twenty-four hours a day instead of one precious hour per week. (#T3844—75¢)

☐ **ROWAN AND MARTIN'S LAUGH-IN #2: MOD MOD WORLD by Roy Doty.** A zany cartoon compendium of all the favorite Laugh-In scenes. (#T3845—75¢)

☐ **THE BROTHERHOOD by Lewis John Carlino.** The compelling drama of two brothers caught in the death-grip of the Mafia. A Paramount Picture starring Kirk Douglas.
(#T3658—75¢)

THE NEW AMERICAN LIBRARY, INC., P.O. Box 2310, Grand Central Station, New York, New York 10017

Please send me the SIGNET BOOKS I have checked above. I am enclosing $_____(check or money order—no currency or C.O.D.'s). Please include the list price plus 10¢ a copy to cover mailing costs. (New York City residents add 5% Sales Tax. Other New York State residents add 2% plus any local sales or use taxes.)

Name_____

Address_____

City_____State_____Zip Code_____

Allow at least 3 weeks for delivery